the Mother-in-Law Dance

Annie Chapman

HARVEST HOUSE PUBLISHERS

EUGENE, OREGON

Cover by Koechel Peterson & Associates, Inc., Minneapolis, Minnesota

Harvest House Publishers has made every effort to trace the ownership of all poems and quotes. In the event of a question arising from the use of a poem or quote, we regret any error made and will be pleased to make the necessary correction in future editions of this book.

THE MOTHER-IN-LAW DANCE
Copyright © 2004 by Annie Chapman
Published by Harvest House Publishers
Eugene, Oregon 97402
www.harvesthousepublishers.com

Library of Congress Cataloging-in-Publication Data

Chapman, Annie.
    The mother-in-law dance / Annie Chapman.
        p. cm.
    ISBN 978-0-7369-1456-7 (pbk.)
    ISBN 978-0-7369-3093-2 (eBook)
    1. Christian women—Family relationships. 2. Mothers-in-law—Religious life. 3. Daughters-in-law—Religious life. 4. Christian women—Religious life. I. Title.
    BV4527.C45 2004
    248.8'43—dc22   2004001048

Printed in the United States of America

13 14 15 16 17 / BP-MS / 15 14 13 12 11

I dedicate this book to those in-laws in my life who have added more love and acceptance than I ever expected or deserved…

To Lillian Chapman
You are and have always been an example of Christ's love and mercy. Thank you for earning the title "Best Mother-in-Law."

To Stephanie Chapman
I knew Nathan had impeccable taste and judgment, but you have proven beyond question his ability to choose wisely. Welcome to the family. All of us love you.

To Emmitt Beall
What a great job Heidi did when she picked you for her husband. You are as dear to me as any son could be. You make loving you the easiest thing I could ever do.

To Paul J. Chapman
You are not only a wonderful father-in-law to me, but you are the anchor of our family. Your children, grandchildren, and great-grand-children look to your life as a clear and unwavering example of the love and acceptance of our heavenly Father. Thank you for being a moral compass we can all follow.

Acknowledgments

Thank you to the hundreds of women who have generously shared their hearts with me. Without your willing participation in filling out questionnaires, speaking to me directly, and sending me personal stories, I could not have written these pages.

Contents

Introduction 7

1. May I Have This Dance? 11

2. Who Is Supposed to Lead? 27

3. Dancing Without Stepping on Toes 41

4. The Dance Floor Is Too Crowded 55

5. Waltzing to Rap Music 67

6. Square Dancing on a Round Floor 85

7. When You Hear a Different Beat 99

8. Boxers Dance, Too 117

9. Trading Partners 133

10. Dance Lessons 149

11. Dance Rehearsals—A Study Guide 159

    Notes 181

Introduction

I love to dance! Truthfully, I'm not any good at it, but I like to try. Most observers would consider my style of movement as "toe dancing." Oh, no, I'm not a ballerina. I just spend most of my time on my dance partner's toes. Regardless of my lack of fluidity, when it comes to dancing one thing is for sure: If I'm going to venture out on the floor to "trip the light fantastic," I want the privilege of picking my dance partner. But that doesn't happen with in-laws.

Mothers-in-law and daughters-in-law are family partners fused together by circumstance and law. To be thrown into a close family relationship without giving consent or being consulted is a daunting challenge. But it's a challenge that can be overcome. The mother-in-law/daughter-in-law relationship is without question a complicated dance. Yet, by the very nature of the relationship, these two women are expected to immediately move freely and beautifully in synchronized harmony. Rarely is this connectedness and closeness realized overnight. In fact, the in-law dance can be a tedious tango. And perhaps some of you have already discovered that a long-lasting, positive relationship requires time, wisdom, compromise, grace, and prayer.

As a daughter-in-law and a mother-in-law, I've been an active dance partner for many years. To help you make your in-law relationship more loving, I offer you my experience in the delicate negotiations and gentle understanding that is required for establishing loving, healthy in-law relationships.

Through hundreds of conversations with women and specially designed questionnaires many more completed, I've garnered some general principles, potential missteps to watch out for, and practical ideas to help you create more positive interactions with your in-law. I'm sure you'll be able to relate to some of their stories and how they've dealt with in-law issues. I have, however, changed names, altered specific details, and lighted edited some comments to protect the privacy and integrity of the women who graciously shared their stories.

In *The Mother-in-Law Dance*, you'll also discover solid biblical principles that will encourage your own spiritual growth and help you get along positively with your mother-in-law or daughter-in-law. Any book on relationships would not be complete without the wisdom from God's Word and the love and grace experienced through a dynamic relationship with His Son, Jesus.

As you discover how to move gracefully in tandem with your in-law, you'll discover that your relationship can be an enjoyable, lifelong adventure as well as an exciting privilege!

The first time I ever met my daughter-in-law was when she was introduced to me as my son's wife. Not only was I shocked by the sudden decision they had made to get married, but I was also emotionally crushed at the reality that I had not been invited to my own son's wedding. I tried, as best I could, to hide my hurt feelings. I can't help but feel that I was cheated out of a day I had dreamed of since my son was a little boy. I wondered, "Is *this* the woman I had prayed for all these years?" I know my son is at fault, too, but it's going to take some time for me to feel right by his wife. I didn't expect him to understand the importance of his wedding day to me because he's never been very sentimental, but I do think his wife should have put herself in my place. Now I have to act like everything is fine and dandy, but it's not.

1
May I Have This Dance?

The candles are lit, the room glows with a soft yellow hue, the groom, the pastor, and the wedding party are in place at the altar. As all eyes eagerly watch the closed door at the chapel's entrance, suddenly the air is changed from the sweet stillness of anticipation to the first notes of the beautiful music chosen for the wedding processional. As the doors swing open, the bride's heart races at the sound of the melodic cue to make that long-awaited, slow walk down the aisle of matrimony. But as the song plays, the lovely bride does not realize that she is not the only lady in the room who has been cued by the music.

Her mother-in-law-to-be is also called to respond to the melody. While the young woman in white moves gracefully with the music toward her chosen one, the song calls the mother of the groom to graciously step to the side. In reality, the wedding processional is not just for the bride, it is also a cue for a lifelong dance to begin for two special women in one man's life.

How true it is that so much changes for a family when the adult children fall in love and marry. Suddenly there are new members who, by decree of law and circumstance, are expected to be embraced and included into the fold. By all means, the challenge is a daunting one, especially for mothers-in-law and daughters-in-law.

Even though the mother-in-law may have had no direct input into her son's decision of who and when to marry, other than years of intense prayer for her child's mate-to-be, the fact remains that the family experience is definitely impacted by the soul-mate selection made by her offspring.

In the same way, the daughter-in-law who may have chosen to join with her husband in holy matrimony has to face the challenge of being joined in a holy alliance with the rest of his family. By the sheer nature of the relationship she is expected to melt into a household of folks that are often unfamiliar and at times very different from her family of origin.

The reality is that every holiday, every special occasion, even the continuance of the coming generations pivot on the choice to unite families through marriage. Whether the parents-in-law or the adult children realize it or not, the choices that are made are life-altering for the entire family.

For most parents, the grace to love and enfold these new family-members-by-law is a mere continuum of the parental love they enjoy with their own kids. However, there are those situations that may require an attitude adjustment. What does a parent do when their child's preference of a mate is contrary to their personality or taste? Or what if the offspring ventures outside of their culture, social class, or religion? Is it possible to accept and even cherish the chosen one when they are an unnatural fit?

And what about the daughter-in-law? What is she supposed to do when she's thrust into a new family that may have already established traditions, modes of interaction, and common activities that perhaps she doesn't readily accept or enjoy? She, along with her mother-in-law, can find comfort in knowing that they are not the first to venture out on that sometimes slippery dance floor.

Love Is Stronger than Differences

There are few biblical references to the mother-in-law/daughter-in-law relationship that can lend us a bird's-eye view of what that kinship should look like. The most well-known in-laws in the Bible are Ruth and Naomi. Without question, the sufficiency of the legendary depth of their love connection can benefit all of us even today. Borrowing from the lovely declaration of commitment to her mother-in-law, brides and grooms for centuries have quoted the words of Ruth. In fact, my husband, Steve, and I used this familiar passage in our own wedding ceremony:

> Do not urge me to leave you or turn back from following you; for where you go, I will go, and where you lodge, I will lodge. Your people shall be my people, and your God, my God. Where you die, I will die, and there I will be buried. Thus may the LORD do to me, and worse, if anything but death parts you and me (Ruth 1:16-17).

In light of the struggle many in-laws experience as they strive to learn to love the one they did not choose, it is ironic that the sweetest words of love recorded in all of antiquity would be between these two in-laws. Why was it so easy for Ruth and Naomi to open their hearts to one another? Was it because they had so much in common? Of all the young maidens available for marriage, was Ruth the choice-bride Naomi would have picked?

Actually, there were extreme differences between these two women, and that is what makes their decision to love one another even more impressive. Naomi was a Jewish woman from a wealthy, prominent family. Ruth was a woman born into a pagan religion and from a poor family. I can only imagine how it must have vexed Naomi's heart to see her sons bring home women who did not share the same religion, traditions, social class, or cultural history.

Did she blame her husband for the lack of suitable Jewish girls for her sons' brides? After all, it was her husband who decided to leave their beloved Bethlehem. Or perhaps she was able to accept these young wives because she was such a gentle soul. Did her sweet demeanor allow her to bridge the differences and embrace her sons' wives as her own daughters?

The biblical text gives us a peek into what kind of person Naomi was. The scriptural account alludes to the fact that she was probably not an easy person to love. And who could blame her. She was a wounded, empty woman who had lost much. After her sons also died and in order to let all those around her know the depth of her pain, Naomi changed her name to explain her plight. She said, "Do not call me Naomi [which means "pleasant"]; call me Mara [meaning "bitter"], for the Almighty has dealt very bitterly with me. I went out full, but the LORD has brought me back empty" (Ruth 1:20-21).

She doesn't sound like the life of the party. Without question she had suffered terrible losses. While living in a foreign land far from friends and family, her husband and two sons had died, leaving her to take care of herself and her daughters-in-law. Not only was she financially poor, but she was also broken in spirit and bitter toward God.

While it may have been a daunting challenge for Naomi to accept one son's choice of a woman who came from outside her culture and class, the fact is, learning to embrace an in-law is not a one-sided affair. Ruth must have recognized the sizable task that awaited her. She was expected to accept and love Naomi as her mother, even though her mother-in-law, filled with disappointment, brought her own set of baggage into the relationship.

History records the fruit of Naomi and Ruth's efforts to bridge the gaps. They were able to overcome their differences, and the Scriptures record that they lived together in harmony. Their "graceful dance" as in-laws established the highest standard of behavior for the rest of us to follow. Despite the brokenness and bitterness of the mother-in-law and the seemingly insurmountable differences of the daughter-in-law, love won out. As a result of the love-bond between them, Ruth became the great-grandmother of King David. Without a doubt, the grace of God crowned their unforgettable relationship by allowing a foreign unbeliever to be placed in the direct lineage of the Messiah, Jesus Christ.

Love Is Stronger than Hurt

Just as Naomi might have chosen a different bride for her son, my friend Janet might have selected a different life-partner for her baby boy. When Janet found out that her son was marrying Pam, she had mixed feelings about the decision. It wasn't that she disliked her. On the contrary, she found Pam to be a loving partner for her son. Pam was not a bad person, she had just had a bad life. Previously married to a man who beat and abused her and her child, she wore her woundedness like a cloak.

Janet had always dreamed of the day when she would fully embrace a daughter-in-law with the same energy and vitality with which she loved her own daughter. The two of them always had the best of times. They could shop-till-they-dropped with the best of them. Laughter and talking rang out throughout the house when they were together. To Janet's way of thinking, adding a daughter-in-law simply meant one more girl with whom to chum around.

However, Pam was not like Janet's daughter. She didn't readily laugh a lot, and she seemed to always isolate herself from the rest of the family. For instance, when the other women were in the kitchen preparing the meal for a family gathering, Pam would sit all alone in the living room quietly leafing through a magazine.

I asked Janet if she encouraged Pam to join them. Her answer demonstrated the patient wisdom she possessed. Janet replied, "No. As much as I would love for Pam to feel comfortable being with me and the rest of the family, I've decided to give her space enough to choose whether she stays in the living room or comes into the kitchen. For too long, she's had someone telling her what to do, and when she didn't do it fast enough, she was punished. I don't want to be another person demanding to have my way. I love her, and I believe in time she will feel that love. Until then, I will continue to be patient and understanding. She's a wonderful wife to my son. That's all she owes me."

Avoiding Regrets

As a result of the time spent with Pam, Janet has learned valuable lessons over the past few years. The two women have since grown amazingly close and continue to do so. This mother-in-law's understanding and kindness has been instrumental in healing the hurts of a lovely young woman. Janet did it right, and she has reaped the joyous benefits of her choices. Others have not fared as well. I asked some mothers-in-law to share what they would consider their biggest regret related to their relationship with their daughters-in-law. Here are some of their thoughts…

- ☺ We've never been able to get on the same page. We think so differently; we have nothing in common.

- ☺ She was not a Christian when she married my son. Things only got more complicated after the grandchildren arrived. I regret that I was not a better Christian witness to her.

- ☺ Everything I do seems to interfere with my son and daughter-in-law. I don't mean to do it, but it seems like I just can't stop myself from offering advice when I think they're doing something wrong. I'm afraid my "over-mothering" has built a thick wall between me and my daughter-in-law.

- ☺ I was never able to convince her that I wanted to be her friend and not her competition.

- ☺ I wish we had been able to overcome our initial awkwardness. We are not close, and I fear we never will be.

- ☺ I speak before I think. That gets me into more trouble than any other fault I have. I don't mean to be rude. Something will be on my mind, and before I can stop it, it's out my mouth. Unfortunately, this fault has caused a lot of pain. My son just ignores me, but my daughter-in-law gets hurt.

- ☺ I've not been as patient as I should be, especially since I'm the older woman and supposed to be the more mature one.

- ⊘ I don't really know my daughter-in-law. They live a long way from us.

- ⊘ Early in the marriage, I confronted her about some things I thought were wrong in her life. That was not smart. It took a long time before she would talk to me.

- ⊘ When they were first married, I was too involved with their lives. When I realized that, I backed off. But I backed away too much. Then they thought I didn't care about them. It's hard to know where the balance is.

- ⊘ I blamed my daughter-in-law for taking my son away from me. My negative attitude drove a wedge between me and her, but also between me and my son. I wish I could start all over with them.

- ⊘ When my daughter-in-law first came into our family, she treated me really bad. My biggest regret is that I treated her bad right back.

I also asked some daughters-in-law to share with me what they would consider the biggest regret they have when it comes to their relationship with their mothers-in-law…

- ⊘ I didn't call to check on her when we were first married. Now, if I started showing concern for her, she'd think I was up to something. I suppose it's too late for us.

- ⊘ I didn't pray for her like I should have.

- ⊘ I didn't hug her or show her affection.

- ⊘ My husband was in the military, so we lived out of state. We allowed too much time to pass before we went to see her. We didn't call very often, either. I guess it's not surprising at all that we're not very close.

- I used my mother-in-law as a babysitter. I took advantage of her.

- I withheld my children from their grandmother. I don't know if she'll ever get over that.

- I didn't tell her I loved her. I wanted to, but that's not how I was raised. There were times when I could tell she wanted me to show her affection, but I didn't.

- I was not patient with her. It was really hard for her to let go of her son. I could have made it easier on her if I would have lightened up a bit.

- I regret that I vented anger about her son to her. Big mistake! No matter how badly he was acting, she didn't want to be put into the position of choosing sides against him.

- I didn't share the message of redemption with her. When she died, I felt really bad. I don't know if she ever gave her heart to Jesus.

- She's so caught up in keeping her house perfect that she doesn't enjoy her grandchildren. I think they're beginning to pick up on her attitude. They don't want to go to her house anymore. She's really missing out, and so are my children.

- I've never been able to feel comfortable in her presence.

- We live way too close to one another. In some ways it's convenient, but in other ways, it's awful.

I offer these confessions and insights so that you can use the experiences of these women to avoid unnecessary regrets.

Love Is Stronger than Feelings

What is a person supposed to do if she honestly doesn't like her in-law? It sounds like a complicated question because there could be any number of valid reasons a person might sternly resist the idea of embracing a mother-in-law or daughter-in-law. But actually, we can turn this into a very simple question: "Should we love everyone?" Are you ready for the answer? Even when we don't feel like loving one another, we should *act like we do!*

Are you asking, "Am I supposed to *pretend* to like someone, even when I can't stand the thought of her? Isn't it wrong to be deceptive and two-faced? Don't I need to be honest with my feelings?" Using the guise of honesty to justify being mean or negative to someone does not demonstrate the character of Christ. Actually, being hateful with a religious label on it is the opposite of who we are supposed to be as ambassadors of Christ.

Let's look at what God's Word says about taking our feelings and emotions under the authority and supervision of the Holy Spirit. In His Word, we will find the way to love even when it doesn't feel right.

In Colossians, chapter 3, we find some of the most incredible instruction for positive Christian living. I want to point out two things found in this passage that will help us love our in-laws, even when our emotions are not cooperating. We are to "put aside" and "put on." Verse 8 lists the things we are to "put aside": "anger, wrath, malice, slander, and abusive speech." The instruction continues in verse 9. We are to stop lying to one another and "put aside" the things we did before we gave our hearts to Christ.

As we read the list of things we are to rid from our lives, there is, then, room for the other character qualities that we are to "put on." (*Note:* We cannot "put on" until we have first "put aside.") I'm really glad God used the concept of "putting on." When I hear that phrase, I automatically think of shopping. While you might agree that it is really fun to go to the mall with a family member or friend to try on dresses, did you realize that when we go into the fitting rooms, we are exercising a deep spiritual lesson? (All the more reason to shop!) When we "put on" clothes, we are covering our nakedness and hiding our shamefulness.

From the first time sin entered into the world through the sin of Adam and the deception of Eve, the need for covering was imprinted on us. As we learn to love one another, we need to be properly attired. What is the suitable outfit for the mother-in-law/daughter-in-law dance? In Colossians 3:12, we are told to "put on" a "heart of compassion, kindness, humility, gentleness and patience." Keep in mind, by the way, that the Scripture *does not* say "God will put on you." Instead, we are instructed to *deliberately* choose this piece of spiritual clothing. We are to "put on" the garment of "bearing with one another, and forgiving each other." If we have a complaint against anyone, we are to forgive that person in the same way God has forgiven our sins. Verse 14 says to "put on love, which is the perfect bond of unity." The result of "putting aside" the dirty garment of hurtful things we do to one another and "putting on" the cloak of kindness is that we can experience what we read in verse 15: "Let the peace of Christ rule in your hearts, to which indeed you were called in one body; and be thankful."

Choosing the truth of God's Word and acting in a loving manner, even when our own feelings may mock us, is the right thing to do. When we reject the temptation to trust in our own fickle feelings and, instead, trust in Christ's heart, then we will be rewarded for that act of faith. God reminds us that "the heart is more deceitful than all else and is desperately sick; who can understand it? I, the LORD, *search the heart*, I *test the mind*, even to give to each man according to his ways, according to the *results of his deeds*" (Jeremiah 17:9-10, emphasis added). God promises us that when we "put aside" those actions that are hurtful and we "put on" a heart attitude that results in kind deeds, He will reward us accordingly.

To give you some practical ideas of how to "put on" love, here are some really beautiful "dresses" that daughters-in-law have suggested for mothers-in-law to put on and model for her family:

- be positive and encouraging
- pray for the young couple
- respect your daughter-in-law's different way of doing things
- let them live their own lives
- no meddling allowed
- send cards and acknowledge important days
- be sensitive about when to share your thoughts and when to be quiet
- give advice only when requested
- don't set too many expectations for your daughter-in-law to meet
- give her time and space
- affirm her every chance you get; compliment her abilities, taste, and character
- be a Christian example to her—not judgmental, but loving
- praise much. Consider criticism poison to the relationship
- don't compare your daughter-in-law to your daughter
- have a sense of humor; don't be afraid to lighten up

And here are some really nice clothes from the mothers-in-law for the daughters-in-law to wear for "the dance":

- love your husband
- be teachable
- be yourself and relax
- love your mother-in-law and tell her you do
- be patient with his mother. It's hard to let go
- pray for your mother-in-law. God can change her even when no one else can
- don't complain about your husband to other people
- keep close to your own family; you need their support
- maintain your personal relationship with Christ. Go to church no matter who else goes with you
- pay attention to your own marriage. Don't get so involved with everyone and everything else that you forget your husband
- don't compare your mother-in-law to your mother. Appreciate both of them and their differences. Just because they may do things differently doesn't mean one is right and the other one is wrong
- tell your mother-in-law how much you love her son and what a good job she did in raising him
- work out holiday schedules well in advance
- give it time and keep your sense of humor

Is your situation seemingly too difficult to "put aside" and "put on"? Some people have incredibly difficult situations they are trying to manage. One mother told me that her daughter had fallen in love with a man who was a known child molester. The two of them married as soon as the daughter turned 18.

The man was old enough to be her father. The mother was so distraught that she nearly lost her mind.

Could anything have been more heartbreaking for a mother than to see her daughter drive away with such an animal? She was in a terrible predicament. What else could she do? Did she accept this man into the family with open arms? To be honest, no. Did she long for the day her daughter would be free from his hold over her? Absolutely. But regardless of how horrible the situation was, the mother realized that if she acted the way she wanted to toward him, she would lose her daughter and any contact with her. The mother swallowed her pride and anger and treated him with the courtesy and kindness she would offer to any stranger. She "put on" love. The outcome of this mother tackling such a monumental challenge of loving the desperately unlovable has proven to be worthwhile. Today she and her daughter remain close. Love has prevailed.

No matter what the situation is, God hears and answers our prayers. He will give us the strength to do what is right according to His Word.

My son is a diabetic. He requires a special diet and constant attention to his health. My daughter-in-law doesn't take his condition as seriously as I think she should. Often, she bakes sweets, which he eats, or she insists on going out to eat at fast-food places. As a result, he's not doing as well physically as he should. Watching my son's health deteriorate is beyond painful to me as his mother. I am furious at my daughter-in-law's lack of maturity and her care for my son. What's my place as a mother-in-law as it pertains to his health?

2

Who Is Supposed to Lead?

The same qualities that make *terrific* mothers to small children are often the exact characteristics that make *terrible* mothers once the children are grown. From the moment I knew I was carrying my son, he became my focus. He took his nourishment from my breast. Attentively, I stood over him at night, making sure he was breathing. I taught him to walk, pulled his baby teeth, taught him to read, and even ran behind him holding him up as he learned to ride his bike.

When he became a teenager, I helped him study the operator's manual and took him to get his learner's permit to drive a car. Each time the orthodontist tightened his braces, I was there to make him Jell-O and listen to his complaints. I worked to save money for his college education and helped him buy his first car. I risked my life giving birth to him, and spent the following years losing sleep, spending money, and even enduring his practical jokes. No one could have loved a son more.

And then one day he got married. All the energy and attention I had directed his way suddenly came to a screeching halt. When he stood next to his bride before the preacher and said "I do," then I was done. At least, that's the way it's supposed to work. But for some it is extremely difficult to turn off the "mommy faucet." The feelings a mother may experience as she releases her son to "the other woman" in his life is captured in this poem:

Who Gives This Man Away?

The laughter and love that filled the room
Fades to her thoughts 'neath a silent moon
"This day has come and gone too soon"
She whispers to herself

Her son once filled her empty arms
Safe in her nest from hunger and harm
But now he finds love in another's charms
And the time has come for farewell

Of all the words that were spoken
On this his wedding day
No one thought about asking her
"Who gives this man away?"

Today, while every eye was on the girl in white
And the music soared like a dove in flight
While love danced in the candlelight
She walked back through the years

She saw a little boy with golden hair
Reaching up and looking scared
It was hard to believe it was him up there
Now, softly fall the tears

Of all the words that were spoken
On this his wedding day
No one thought about asking her
"Who gives this man away?"

But she'll be strong
And she'll hide it well
But she knows
It's gonna be a hard farewell[1]

A mature daughter-in-law will recognize the inherent challenge her mother-in-law faces and offer patient understanding

as she learns to let go. Without question, both women have adjustments that must be made. The young daughter-in-law is learning to be a wife to her husband, and the mother-in-law is learning how to "unmother" her son. Both jobs can be difficult. Each woman deserves ample amounts of loving patience. With that in mind, the obvious question that remains when it comes to the mother-in-law/daughter-in-law dance is "Who is supposed to lead?"

Who Is the Leader?

Regardless of how difficult the transitions for both mother-in-law and daughter-in-law may be, the fact remains that the "dance" will go on. One of the first decisions that must be made when learning to dance together is "Who is going to lead?" If both dancers insist on that powerful position, confusion and chaos is the only possible outcome. Before long, one or the other is going to trip and fall. In the mother-in-law/daughter-in-law dance, the leader is not the one who takes over and directs the action. Instead, the leader in this fragile shuffle *steps back* and gets out of the way. Without question, the leader in this waltz should be the mother-in-law. She is the one who lets go and lovingly releases her son and his wife to establish their own lives and routine.

What Does Leading Look Like?

If the mother-in-law is effectively leading, it is often revealed by her reaction when she sees her son and his wife making decisions that she may or may not approve of. What if, for example, the newlywed husband and his wife want to go to a different church than the one the family has traditionally attended? What if they don't want to come over every Sunday

for lunch? What if they want to have the option of going out
with their friends for dinner instead of always coming to the
in-laws when they have a free evening? By backing away and
supporting their choices, the mother-in-law gives the new
family the freedom to be separate in a peaceful, constructive
manner. This act of love demonstrates not only her maturity,
but it also eliminates the need for her son and his wife to cut
themselves off in a more radical manner.

Years ago, when our children were very young, my husband and I anticipated the day when love would demand that
we let go of our precious ones. The following lyric was written
with that time in mind.

The Arrow and the Bow

Here is wisdom for the moms and dads
That time has proven true
The day your children learn to walk away
They start to walk away from you

For at first, you hold all of them
Cradled safely in your arms
Then one day, their hand is all you'll hold
And soon, it's just their heart

And there'll even come the time
If your love for them is true
You'll have to let their hearts go free
To let them love someone else not only you

Can the sparrow ever learn to fly
If the nest is all it knows
Can the arrow ever reach its mark
By remaining in the bow
You have to let it go...[2]

The Wrong Way to Lead

I asked hundreds of daughters-in-law from all over the country to share what it feels like when the mother-in-law refuses to lead by letting go. The frustrations and hurt feelings were quite evident in the replies they offered. Here are a few of the representative heartfelt responses to the question "What did your mother-in-law do wrong, and how did it make you feel?"

- ☉ She criticized my cooking....It made me feel inadequate, and eventually I quit cooking.

- ☉ When my husband and I first married I got strep throat. My mother-in-law was more concerned with her son being exposed than the fact that I was seriously ill. She never offered to bring food or help in any way. I felt like she really didn't love me at all.

- ☉ Because of my husband's parents being divorced, I married into a situation with two mothers-in-law. My husband's stepmother wouldn't attend our wedding because the first wife was going to be there. She made my father-in-law choose between his son and her.

- ☉ She would laugh and make fun of me and the children because we were Christians....It made me feel belittled....She considered something important to me as if it were nothing.

- ☉ She invites my husband and me to come to dinner when she knows I'm working. She likes it when it's just the original four of her family—the way it used to be without any "outsiders."...It hurts my feelings and makes me feel like I'll never be a part of the family.

- ☉ She disliked me through four years of dating and five years of marriage because I was divorced and overweight....It made me feel hurt, angry, and resentful.

⊙ She challenged my mothering and authority in front of the children. She told dirty jokes, had vulgar talk, and smoked in front of them....It made me feel angry and resentful.

⊙ She was my teenage daughter's alibi. She lied to me so my daughter could sneak around behind my back and date a man who was not only 20 years older than my daughter, but was married to another woman at the time. To my horror, my daughter married the man and wasted 5 years of her life. If my mother-in-law had not interfered, my daughter might not have ruined her life.

⊙ She interfered constantly in our early years of marriage. We moved five hours away. That helped somewhat....I felt like I was living on a battlefield.

⊙ Even though she has been divorced from her husband for 25 years, she still makes her adult children choose between her and their father....I feel like I am dealing with a "spoiled child" who has an absolute stranglehold on my husband. We have to sneak around to visit with my father-in-law....I don't know what to do about the situation short of starting a major war in the family.

⊙ She comes uninvited into my own home and tells me how to arrange my furniture, what to cook for dinner, and how to discipline my children....I feel inadequate, nervous, and self-conscious.

⊙ She didn't teach my husband to clean up after himself....As a result I am overworked....It's like having an additional, extra-messy child in the home.

⊙ She didn't come to visit us often enough....I felt sad and thought I was missing out on getting to know someone really special.

⊙ She was abusive and hot tempered.

⊙ For some reason she would never listen to me or my opinion….It made me feel unimportant.

⊙ She would try to get my husband to do something with her after I already had plans to be with him….By using guilt and manipulation, she would make him choose between the two of us. I told him it was okay to do what his mother wanted because I didn't want to put him on the spot…. Eventually, he learned to tell her no without too much emotional stress.

⊙ She came to the wedding from a country overseas, and then stayed for the next six weeks. She even went on the honeymoon with us! It made me feel jealous and resentful.

Leading the Right Way

I asked daughters-in-law to share how it feels when the mother-in-law leads by backing away and allowing her son's family the right to live independently. The question was "What is one thing your mother-in-law did right?" The following are some of the responses offered by the younger generation of women. As I read them, I was encouraged with what a great job many of the older women had done or are doing.

My mother-in-law…

⊙ loved me from the start and made me feel a part of the family.

⊙ treated me like a beloved daughter and introduced me to others as such.

⊙ took an active, yet not overbearing role in the life of my children.

⊙ is good to her son and treats him with respect as a man. She doesn't act like he's a little boy or try to mother him anymore.

⊙ came to our children's special activities when she was able.

- ⊙ taught my husband to be respectful of woman and to see them as his equal.

- ⊙ included me in the family gatherings, and let me be a part of the planning.

- ⊙ loaned us money so we could buy our first house. We couldn't have done it without my in-laws. (We paid them back!)

- ⊙ was visiting us and saw me getting behind with my work. She pitched in and did dishes, laundry, held the baby.... She was a great help to me.

- ⊙ tells me she loves me. I come from a family that is less demonstrative with hugs and words. Now that I'm used to it, I really like it.

- ⊙ has been a wonderful example of what a loving wife should be toward her husband. I've learned so much from her just watching her interact with her family.

- ⊙ has taught me a lot about keeping house. When we got married, I didn't know how to cook and clean. At my insistence, she's been my teacher.

- ⊙ has lived out the Christian life and has been an incredible blessing. I don't really know anyone who is as consistent a Christian as she is.

- ⊙ never interferes or offers unwanted advice.

- ⊙ has always been there for me since the first day I met her. She did my hair on my wedding day. She was there with my parents when my children were born. We've shared colicky babies, prayer requests, laughter, tears, and recipes. But most of all, we've shared a love for God and for our families. I am blessed with two wonderful mothers—mine and my husband's.

A group of young daughters-in-law were discussing the complexities of the in-law relationship when one of the girls asked the question, "Why is it so much more difficult for a mother to let go of her son than it is for her to release her daughter? My mom and I are just as close now as we were before I got married. But she's having a really tough time letting my brother and his wife establish their own family."

That's a very pertinent question. The reason it's harder for a mom to let a married son go as opposed to a married daughter is quite simple. The mother never lets go of her daughter. The relationship between a mother and her daughter really doesn't change that much when she marries. Of course, there are some necessary adjustments, but for the most part, they still have a direct connection. However, when the son marries, the mom has to let him go completely. In a real sense, she loses her son. Most of us have heard the old adage "A daughter is a daughter for the rest of your life, but a son is a son until he takes a wife." There's a lot of truth in that old saying. A mother's relationship with her son changes because she must go through the daughter-in-law to get to her son. Whether a mother likes it or not, there's another woman in her son's life. And the biblical mandate of "leaving and cleaving" shifts the power to the son's wife and away from his mother.

A sensitive daughter-in-law who acknowledges the fact that getting along with her mother-in-law will help create a better life for her and her husband will strive to understand just how difficult the letting go process really is for the mother. My husband, Steve, wrote the following poem for me and my son at the time of Nathan's high school graduation. It illustrates some of the feelings a mother experiences as she sees her son leaving.

Dance with the One

Before you go dancing out of our lives
Son, there's a dance you must do

With the prettiest girl at your party tonight
She's looking this way at you

Go on over to her, and ask her in style
And I'll clear a place on the floor
Just like you did, when you were a child
Dance with your mother once more

Dance with the one who brought you here
Who loved you the most, through all of these years
Hold her hand gently and remember the tears
Before you tell her goodbye
Dance one more time
With the one who brought you here[3]

Acknowledging Limitations

A dedicated mother is like a mighty river. She is teeming with life, supplying a sense of serenity and calm to all those around her. She supports the heavy barges that are used to move burdens from one place to another. In fact, whenever the adventurous pioneers were settling this great nation, one of the deciding factors whether a home or business should be built in a certain location was determined by its proximity to a river.

The same powerful water supply that is needed to feed, wash, and transport a community is the same vigorous force that can also destroy property, erode banks, flood crops, and drown innocent life. What is it that changes the river from a wonderful asset to a dangerous hazard? It is when the river escapes the boundaries, or banks, that it becomes a deadly liability to those around it. Like the waters of the river, no one does more good than a mother who stays within her boundaries. In the same manner, no one is more destructive than the mom who strays beyond her banks.

The Power of Words

One of the most constructive ways a mother can stay within her boundaries is by containing the mighty force of the tongue. You will notice that the use and misuse of words will be a recurring topic throughout this book. Coming back time and time again to the "tongue theme" is not an original idea. Throughout nearly every book in the Bible, reference is made to what we say and the good or evil that brings. For instance, we are often warned in the Old Testament book of Proverbs concerning the power and the use of the tongue. For example, in Proverbs 10:19 we are admonished, "When there are many words, transgression is unavoidable, but he who restrains his lips is wise." That particular verse is especially proven true when it comes to containing the number of words we use in our relationship with our married children. Keeping our words to a minimum is one of the smartest ways to stay out of trouble. In fact, most any response that needs to be addressed can be summed up with three individual words. Those words are "sure," "really," and "wow."

For instance, your son and his wife come to you and say, "Mom, I know we don't have the money to pay our rent this month and we're behind on some other bills, but we feel like we need to, like, get away and you know, just chill out. So, we've decided to use that new credit card we just got in the mail and go to Hawaii for a nice vacation."

Everything inside you wants to scream, "You have got to be kidding! Are you insane? There is *no way* on this green earth that you can go on vacation right now! What about work? Do you think money grows on trees? If you think I'm going to feed your dog, you'd better think again. Who's going to teach

your Sunday school class? And where's the money you owe
me for your college education?" That's what an unwise mother
who is overflowing her banks might say. But that's not how a
smart, contained mother responds. What is our comeback to
that interesting idea? We look them straight in the eye, swallow
hard, and say, "Really? Wow. Really!" See how easy it is when
you keep your reaction to a one- or two-word response?

Now, just in case that same son and his wife come to you at
the end of the month sporting a beautiful tan and looking rather
rested after their nice vacation and say to you, "You know, Mom,
like we're a little short this month, money-wise, you know. How
about helping us with our rent? What do ya say, Mom?" Going
back to the advice just given, it may be necessary to add one
other word to your response. "Really? Wow. Nope."

I realize that there are some situations that one of those key
words might not fit. In those times feel free to use the old
"hmmm," accompanied by a pondering nod of the head. One
mother said she responds using the same four words. No matter
what is said, she replies, "You *might* be right."

All joking aside, consider yourself forewarned. That little
fleshly member that rests right behind your lips, if allowed to
wag at will, will do more damage than any raging river. In
Proverbs 14:1 we read, "The wise woman builds her house,
but the foolish tears it down with her own hands." That verse
is true, but may I be so bold to add that it's not just her hands
that can destroy a home, but also her tongue?

A mature, godly mother-in-law will find the strength to lead
in the dance with her daughter-in-law. If she really loves her
son, she will back off and recognize the God-given position
that the daughter-in-law now holds. No matter how difficult
it may be, that is the right thing to do.

In the opening story of this chapter, a concerned mother cried out regarding her son's serious health condition. This mother is asking a question that many others share. What is my place as a mother-in-law as it pertains to my son's health? The answer may seem harsh, but it is true, nonetheless. The person who is responsible for the son's health is not his mother or his wife. Oh, yes! The daughter-in-law should be supportive and helpful to her husband. She should not make his choices more difficult by placing tempting morsels in his way. However, when it's all boiled down, no one is accountable for the son's health but him. Should the mother interject herself into this health-care situation? As difficult as it may be, the answer is no.

But what if the son or his wife asks the mother-in-law for some suggestions on how to regulate his medical condition? Following the sound advice offered in Proverbs 16, she should keep in mind that "the wise in heart will be called understanding, and sweetness of speech increases persuasiveness.... The heart of the wise instructs his mouth and adds persuasiveness to his lips. Pleasant words are a honeycomb, sweet to the soul and healing to the bones" (verses 21,23-24).

Keeping her advice brief and sweet will be the best plan for helping a son and his wife through a difficult situation. And if they do not ask for help, then a mother-in-law would be wise to pray and ask God to send information and inspiration to them through some other source.

I'm absolutely crushed. I wanted to love and treat my daughter-in-law the same way I love and treat my daughter. I don't know of anything I did to her, but for some reason she hates me. She questions my motives every time I try to reach out to her. What can I do to change this painful situation? I know my son can feel the tension between us, but he doesn't do anything about it. I hate him being caught in the middle. It kills me to feel the wall she's built between the two of us.

3

Dancing Without Stepping on Toes

One of the consequences of learning to dance is the risk it presents to the dance partner. Without malice or ill intentions, often toes are bruised. Embarrassing moments are simply part of the process of beginning—and even intermediate—dancing. Learning to relate to one another as mother-in-law and daughter-in-law poses the same type of hazard. Out of ignorance and discomfort at the situation, sometimes things are said or done that may offend one or the other.

Some of the best advice I ever received concerning my relationship with my daughter-in-law was given to me by my daughter, Heidi. One day she said, "Mom, don't treat Stephanie like you treat me." My first and immediate reaction to that admonition was a slacked jaw, stunned expression because that was exactly how I intended to treat my "new daughter." However, Heidi continued in spite of my visual recoil. "She *has* an incredible mother. She doesn't need another one. You should get to know her and not assume she thinks like me or likes what I like." I was most grateful for this sound wisdom.

How do we learn to do the in-law dance without seriously hurting our partners or getting hurt ourselves? First, we must accept the fact that there will be blunders. In the face of the likelihood that our humanness will trip us up, the willingness to be forgiving of ourselves and also of each other is paramount to maintaining love between partners.

Careless Words

In response to the question "What, if anything, has your mother-in-law done that hurt your feelings?" a woman who had been married more than 30 years gave an answer that was swift and sure. "On my wedding day I overheard my mother-in-law telling her sister that she thought I looked fat in my wedding gown."

You could almost feel the hurt radiating from this daughter-in-law as she offered her response to a long-ago offense. Sadly, her mother-in-law, saying something she thought was out of her daughter-in-law's hearing, damaged their relationship before it even started with a rude and unnecessary comment. Though she was not aware that her daughter-in-law-to-be was close by, what could she have done to avoid any possibility of inflicting a wound on their relationship? She could have remembered the old adage "a closed mouth gathers no foot" or she could have taken the following simple test.

Putting Our Words to the Test

Years ago someone shared with me the "test" of whether something needs to be said. The three questions we should always ask before opening our mouths are: Is what I'm going to say true? Is it kind? Is it necessary? If the mother-in-law in the previous story had put her "fat comment" to this test, no doubt years of hard feelings could have been avoided.

Our tongues are tattletales. They broadcast to those around us the words that are in our hearts. Jesus offers this warning, as recorded in Matthew 15:18 NIV: "But the things that come out of the mouth come from the heart, and these make a man 'unclean.'" In Matthew 12:34 NLT, Jesus said, "For whatever is in your heart determines what you say. A good person produces good words from a good heart, and an evil person produces evil words from an evil heart. And I tell you this, you must give an account on judgment day of every idle word you speak."

I once heard our words described as feathers. Just imagine taking a feather pillow up on top of a mountain. Cut it open and let the stuffing fly away with the wind. When we say things that are hurtful and damaging to others, those words are like the feathers in the pillow. Once they are airborne, they cannot be retrieved. We can say we're sorry all we want, but we can't take back the words that have been spoken. The best way to keep our words from inflicting unintentional harm is to keep them in our mouths.

Guarding Our Words; Covering with Love

A mother-in-law shared with me her traumatic dilemma. While this story is not uncommon, she offered some of the best advice I've ever heard concerning how to handle this all-too-familiar situation for some families. Much to her sorrow, her son had impregnated his girlfriend. The expectant couple was very young and unsure about whether they should get married. The boy's parents were high-profile leaders in the community. It didn't take long for the word to get out that there was trouble in paradise. All eyes were on this family to see how they would handle the embarrassing predicament.

Before long, the tension grew in the family to the point that injurious words and insinuations began to fly. The son lashed out in anger at the girlfriend. Her family began to accuse the young man of shirking his responsibilities. Even the boy's siblings, who were hurt and disappointed in their older brother, entered into the fray. Words ripped through both families like daggers and stuck like barbs.

Distressed by the ugly tone that rose from her family, the mother of the son gathered her family members in the living room. First, she gave no verbal excuses for her son's immoral and reckless behavior. She was just as upset as any of them that he and his girlfriend had inflicted their lack of restraint on an innocent little baby and had embarrassed their families. Nonetheless, she boldly addressed everyone in the room: "The hateful speech and judgmental slander will end right now. There will be *no* bad-mouthing of this young girl. Not *one* word of negativity will be tolerated in this family. All speculation of intent or assumed motives will cease." In other words, the mother put an end to the destructive presence of gossip in the family.

From that moment on, if a family member couldn't say something good, he or she was expected to keep quiet. (See Philippians 4:8.) The look on the mother-in-law's face when she began to tell me the result of her declaration announced that a victory had been won and love had not been lost. She said, "Some months after my sweet little grandson was born, our two youngsters got married. Our daughter-in-law came into our family and, thankfully, not one of us had to offer apologies for unkind, untrue, or unnecessary words against her."

The stern wisdom of the matriarch of the family had set the standard of compassion, and the rest of the members had followed her lead. The mother-in-law concluded, "By controlling our tongues, we avoided so much sin in our house. Our family motto became, 'Be careful what you say, and get on your knees and pray!'"

What an incredible story from a wonderful, brave woman. If families would eliminate gossip, reject judgment, and season conversations with good, wholesome communication, think what a pleasant and safe place all of our homes would be. One of my favorite poems is a simple reminder of how our words can make a difference in our lives and also in the lives of others. These words were written by an unknown author who found the key to saying much in a few lines.

Power of Words

A careless word may kindle strife
A cruel word may wreck a life
A bitter word may hate instill
A brutal word may smite and kill

A gracious word may smooth the way
A joyous word may light the way
A timely word may lessen stress
A loving word may heal and bless

Avoid Hurtful Words and Deeds

Without question, no one likes to be on the receiving end of unkind and thoughtless statements. A daughter-in-law shared how uncomfortable it can be when you realize you are the one who is holding the sword that is dripping with emotional blood. Sadly, she reported that she was not the one who was offended, but the one who unintentionally inflicted the pain.

Receiving word that her own father was taken suddenly and seriously ill, and with only a couple of days she could spend away from her three young children, she made the last-minute arrangements to go to her hometown and assist her siblings in caring for her dad.

Both this woman's father and in-laws lived in the same small town. Caught up in the emotion of her father's illness and the time crunch of such a brief visit, the young woman failed to call or contact her in-laws while she was in town. Though the daughter-in-law had no intention of slighting her mother-in-law, unfortunately that's exactly what happened.

The night before she was to leave she suddenly realized her oversight and frantically placed the call to say a quick hello to her in-laws. Little did this daughter-in-law expect what happened. The audible reaction on the other end of the phone was heartbreaking. The mother-in-law, hearing that her daughter-in-law was in town, had waited for her to come by to see her. When this expected visit didn't happen, some seriously hurt feelings resulted. The offended mother-in-law cried uncontrollably on the other end of the line, and the daughter-in-law realized to her horror that she was talking to a wounded woman.

The young lady admitted to me, "I was so disgusted with myself. How could I have been so thoughtless? I honestly thought about going to the airport, getting on a plane, and simply disappearing into oblivion. I've never felt like such a failure. I was also dreading my husband's reaction to my social blunder. What was he going to say about me hurting his mother so terribly? But when I saw him at the airport, his words were a healing balm to my ragged heart. I think he actually kept me from 'falling on my own sword.' He tenderly said, 'Don't worry about this, Honey. This could happen to anyone. Mom will just have to get over this. When she can look past her own hurt feelings, she'll see that you never intended to wound her. You have so much on your mind, I can't believe you remembered to do anything. I know you didn't mean to hurt anyone.'"

The daughter-in-law continued, "Even though my mother-in-law did eventually graciously forgive me and, thankfully, my husband cut me some slack, one thing is for sure. I never want to be responsible for hurting anyone like that again."

Sometimes inadvertent hurts are not so quickly forgiven. Diane, a daughter-in-law for more than 30 years, told me about a heartbreaking oversight that has caused incredible harm in her family. The offense took place at an event that is supposed to engender feelings of warmth and closeness. The blunder took place at her son's wedding.

At a point in the picture taking, the photographer asked for the grandmothers of the groom to come onto the platform and be photographed with the newlyweds. Since Diane's mother was in her nineties and in very poor health, she went down to assist her in the navigation of the stairs at the bottom of the platform. Unwittingly, Diane failed to turn around and specifically invite her mother-in-law to join them. She assumed that her in-law was not only capable of climbing the stairs but was also able to follow the instructions the photographer had given them. In her concern for her aging mother, Diane was unaware that she had slighted her mother-in-law and, unknowingly, embarrassed her in front of the wedding party.

During the busyness of the day, Diane was not aware of the cold shoulder that she was getting from her in-laws. But before the bride and groom had left for their honeymoon, she was made aware of how hurt and offended her husband's mother was. The father-in-law took it upon himself to "ream her out" at the reception.

Through gritted teeth, he gruffly said, "How dare you treat my wife with such blatant disregard. What did she ever do to you to warrant such rude, hateful behavior?" He continued his tirade of accusing words. Finally he stopped.

"I couldn't believe that my mother-in-law had taken such an offense over something that was so insignificant and unintentional," Diane said. "I tried to apologize many times, but it's been three years and my in-laws have yet to forgive me. I am the family outcast now. My mother-in-law has turned everyone against me."

These two sad stories highlight the truth that in-law relationships are very fragile and require tender loving care.

Keeping It Clean

Dealing with the hurts that come our way through this delicate mother-in-law/daughter-in-law relationship is necessary if we are to grow in love. As I spoke to the women whose stories are offered in this chapter, I was reminded of an illustration from years ago that is a commentary on how important it is to resolve unpremeditated hurts.

My friend left her clothes dryer on while she made a quick trip to the grocery store. When she returned home the entire house was engulfed in flames. I never heard the final conclusion of why the dryer caught fire. My speculation was that the cause of the tragedy was a neglected lint trap. When we fail to clear out the lint trap, the collection of debris becomes a wad of "kindling," a fire waiting to happen.

Just like accumulating lint, when it comes to personal relationships if we allow little bits and pieces of hurt to pile up in our hearts, then spontaneous combustion can happen at the most inappropriate times.

Collective hurts show up disguised in the strangest of costumes. One daughter-in-law said, "My mother-in-law chose to let her 'lint trap' ignite at my father-in-law's funeral. How did she voice her accumulation of hurts? She refused to allow my parents to attend the final service for my husband's father. I knew she was jealous of my folks, but I couldn't believe she'd make an issue at such an inappropriate and sorrowful time. I seriously thought about not attending the funeral, but that would have only added to my husband's pain. As it turned out, my parents came in spite of her unreasonable objection."

Letting "little things" build up in a clothes dryer can have devastating consequences. But allowing unresolved, unintentional hurts to collect can burn to the ground the fragile relationship between two women who love the same man. Correctly and quickly dealing with conflicts can be the key to avoiding disaster.

The following responses give an important glimpse at some of the combustible litter that exists in the hearts of mothers- and daughters-in-law. Perhaps some of these may sound familiar to you. Daughters-in-law were asked to finish this sentence: If I could, I would tell my mother-in-law to stop...

- ⊙ changing plans once they've been made.
- ⊙ being self-focused and controlling.
- ⊙ interfering by presuming she can plan the schedule of my husband and children without consulting with me.
- ⊙ rearranging my furniture and reorganizing my kitchen when she comes to see us.
- ⊙ making comments about my housekeeping, parenting, and weight.
- ⊙ spoiling my children with money and things.
- ⊙ being nosy and trying to get information about our lives through our children.

⊙ talking badly about my children to other relatives.

⊙ giving unwanted financial advice.

⊙ making her son feel guilty because she was a single mother.

⊙ smoking around my children and in our house.

⊙ fixing dinner for my husband when I'm expecting him to eat with us.

⊙ pressuring us to have children.

⊙ butting in and giving unsolicited advice.

⊙ criticizing my husband.

⊙ showing favoritism to her daughter and her children.

⊙ rolling her eyes in disgust when we tell her we're going to have another baby.

⊙ being dependent on my husband to do all the repairs around her house.

⊙ holding grudges.

⊙ calling the house and asking to speak with my husband. At least say hello to me and stop acting like I don't exist.

⊙ coming over without calling first.

Mother-in-laws were asked to finish this sentence: If I could, I would ask my daughter-in-law to stop...

⊙ being lazy and cook breakfast for your children.

⊙ resisting going to church with your family.

⊙ giving me the silent treatment. How can I get to know you if you won't talk to me?

⊙ looking at me as competition. I want your marriage to be a success.

⊙ treating my husband and me like an ATM machine.

- using me to babysit when you want me to, but not allowing me to take the children when I want to do something special with them.

- refusing to attend family functions that I've scheduled.

- being so mean to my son.

- spending money your family doesn't have. My son is working himself to death to make money you're squandering away.

- having babies you can't take care of.

- keeping my son from coming to see us.

- letting your husband (my son) treat you so disrespectfully.

- comparing me to your mother.

- being unforgiving and impatient with other people.

- spending so much time working and invest more time with your family.

- talking about me in a negative way to your mother and sisters.

Wow! We've just read some brutally honest and very sad statements from the mothers-in-law and daughters-in-law who answered the survey. It is important to keep in mind that they were asked to share specifically the things they found most hurtful in their relationship. And giving them the benefit of the doubt, some of the rude and thoughtless things listed may have been done or said in ignorance. Not intending to insult someone, however, does not always lessen the sting of the comment. But unintentional hurts are a sad reality when it comes to human relationships.

On the other hand, there are many comments spoken and things done to one another that should have been made right. Without question, asking for forgiveness for the unkind, untrue, and unnecessary words is definitely in order. In fact, there will always be a need, as long as we are alive, to offer forgiveness for errant things done and said, as well as to forgive others when they have wronged us. It is not a matter of if we will offend, but when.

As much as we hope we can do it perfectly, we will more than likely step on each other's toes. Just because the preacher pronounces the son and his wife "as one" doesn't mean that it's an automatic fit for the mother-in-law and daughter-in-law. We must allow ourselves some time to get to know one another. And bear in mind that no dancer that I'm aware of ever died from a bruised toe.

I didn't know when I married my husband that his parents would be such an ever-present part of our lives. Not long after we married, my husband and I were transferred to another city. I was secretly excited when I found out we had to move, even though it meant moving away from my own family. Unfortunately, my elation was short-lived when my in-laws followed us to the next town. Now, I feel like part of a sitcom with the intrusive mother-in-law right in my backyard. She spoils my children by giving them stuff and steals our family time. How do I get my life back without hurting her feelings and making my husband mad at me?

4

The Dance Floor Is Too Crowded

We can warn a young couple over and over that marriage is not between two people, but rather it is the uniting of two families. But in the fresh glow of "young love," the caution light is rarely heeded. Perhaps they have bought into the "love can conquer all" mentality. If that be the case, it won't be long before they will face the harsh reality that joining two families is not always pretty or pleasant. Anyone who's been married longer than one Christmas season knows that adjusting to a spouse's family is not necessarily the easiest of jobs. And what happens when the holidays never end? What is a young wife supposed to do when she discovers that her mother-in-law is not an occasional, welcomed visitor, but rather a constant intruder who is worse than a nosy next-door neighbor?

On the flip side of that challenge, how does a mother-in-law cope with the emotions that arise from being treated like she's nothing more than a neighborhood diner, good for a free meal, and a drop-by babysitting service? Is there a way for families to live close to one another without stepping on each other's toes?

Holding the Line

Earlier this year I found out the hard way why property lines exist. Much to my displeasure, I noticed that a lilac bush

I had planted in my garden a few seasons earlier had taken on the appearance and the dimensions of a small tree. The space I had allotted for the eager shrub was not able to accommodate its expanding girth. The remedy was simple; I needed to transplant the bush to another location. Moving the entire tree to a new place was not an easy task. Since it was so heavy, I decided to drag it to the nearest spot capable of containing the large plant. The decision was made. I would plant it along the property line between our lot and our backyard neighbor's place.

I put the shovel deep into the willing soil and lifted the chunk of dirt out of the ground. When I looked into the freshly dug hole, to my chagrin I noticed a black, cablelike wire severed into two pieces. *Oh no!* As I contemplated what had happened, I realized my planting event was over. What had I done? Eventually I discovered that I had cut the cable for our neighbor's television and Internet service. I had made a miscalculation. What I thought was our property really belonged to our neighbor. By stepping over the line, I had disrupted their lives. Graciously, our nearby resident accepted my apology and, to my relief, the cable was easily fixed. Unfortunately, when we disregard the boundaries between our families, too often things are severed that cannot be so easily mended.

The old adage "Fences make good neighbors" is never more true than when it comes to living close to family. Too often the boundary lines get blurred and hearts and feelings are bruised. One experienced daughter-in-law generously shared with me her story of what it was like to live much too close, for much too long, to her mother-in-law. The following is her account of 37 years of living on a crowded dance floor.

Setting Boundaries Without Building Walls

When my husband and I got married, in my ignorance I agreed to buy a house right next door to my mother-in-law. In all honesty, this was not fair to either of us. Since things had not changed that much, my mother-in-law saw no need to alter how she related to her son. To my disadvantage, she didn't make the connection between her son getting married and her responsibilities coming to an end. The only thing different in her thinking was now that he was married he simply lived next door and not in the next room. That was merely a small inconvenience.

From the beginning there were absolutely no boundaries between the two homes. At her will, she would enter without knocking. Anytime she had an opinion, she gave it a voice. She picked which church we attended. She was outspoken about how we spent our money, where we went on vacation, and how we raised our children.

If I had been a mean wife and hateful mother, perhaps I could have understood her stepping in to rescue her son and his children. But the truth is, I did a wonderful job with my family. I took great pride in serving them and creating a loving environment in our home. Her criticisms were totally unjustified. There was no reason for her to treat me so badly.

I tried everything to gain her approval and respect. I learned to cook her recipes (sometimes they tasted better than when she cooked them). I grew a large and fruitful garden and shared the vegetables with her.

Since she didn't drive a car, I would rearrange my day so I could take her to the doctor when she had an appointment or needed medical attention. Putting my own schedule aside, every week I would drive her to get her groceries. But all of my attempts to show her love were met at best with cold indifference and at worst, open hostility. After so many years of trying, I finally realized that trying to gain her love and acceptance was nothing more than an exercise in futility. Withholding her praise and approval was just her way of controlling me.

Sadly enough, she never offered me her love and affection, not even when she was dying. Even though I've never felt such pain and rejection, I eventually came to realize that she was the one to be pitied. She voluntarily cut herself off from someone who truly cared about what happened to her.

There was a twist to the competitive nature of my relationship with my mother-in-law that I find baffling, even to this day. There were times when I got the feeling she was jealous of any affection my husband gave to me. It was as though she was in a romantic rivalry with me. Living day in and day out with such a person, I've concluded that there's probably not a more unattractive relationship than a jealous mother-in-law and an insecure wife.

Being a Christian, I was able to fight through the hurt feelings in order to keep my eyes on the goal. I couldn't let how she behaved change who I wanted to be. My objective was to be able to live in such a way that I could look myself in the mirror and see the image of

Christ being formed in me daily. I once read, "We are never more like God than when we are forgiving a wrong." Well, God must have really wanted me to be like Him. He gave me many opportunities to forgive on a regular basis.

I was able to survive living next door to my in-laws. I have two other sisters-in-law (my husband's brother moved in on the other side of his parents) who didn't fare as well. My mother-in-law drove them away. Looking back, I see that many of the problems rested squarely on the shoulders of the men in the family. Did my husband come to my rescue when I was being shredded by his mother's cutting comments and intrusive behavior? There were a few times when he sought to corral his mother. But most of the time he just took care of himself because, too often, he was on the receiving end of her hateful demeanor.

Without question, we should have moved farther away from my in-laws when we realized what kind of situation we were in. But there were too many extenuating circumstances that entered into the equation. So, foolishly we continued to live next door. My husband and his brother could not find it in themselves to "cut the apron strings," or should I say the umbilical cord. What was it about those boys that they could not live more than a few feet away from their mother? I wish I knew!

Regardless of the difficulties I have endured at the hands of an overbearing mother-in-law who never learned to let go of her son, I am now, without question, the best mother-in-law in the history of the world! I suppose, in all fairness, that really isn't up to me to decide whether I'm doing a better job. Only my daughter-in-law can attest to that fact.

The reason I am so determined to be a good mother-in-law is that I know what it feels like to be on the receiving end of unkind words and unjustifiable judgments. As a result of that kind of treatment, I never want to make my daughter-in-law feel the way I have felt. My prayer is that my children will be the benefactors of the years I spent with my in-laws.

By the way, my son figured out that the biblical mandate to a husband is a great idea. When it says in Matthew 19:5, "For this reason a man shall leave his father and mother and be joined to his wife, and the two shall become one flesh," it really means it. As a result, he and his family live 200 miles away from us. Perhaps he learned as much from my experience as I did.

Never Too Late to Start?

As I listened to this lovely lady tell her sad story, I kept thinking about how different her life could have been if she and her husband had established some basic boundaries from the beginning of their marriage. Perhaps everyone would have acted more responsibly if there had been some guidelines to live within. It may seem strange, but it is so very true: We train others how to treat us. When we accept other people's ill behavior, we are actually reinforcing it and encouraging them to repeat it.

Can we establish boundaries and still be nice people? Is letting others walk over us demonstrating Christ's life and love in us? Is allowing ourselves to be disrespected what Jesus requires in His wonderful Sermon on the Mount? Are we naive when we expect those around us to treat us with courtesy and kindness? The response to these perplexing questions can be summed up in a simple answer Jesus gave in Matthew 7:12: "Therefore, treat people the same way you want them to treat you, for this is the Law and the Prophets." How do we want to be treated? Personally, I want to have boundaries. I want to know where the "property lines" fall. It makes life so much more productive when we can work within general guidelines.

Even though it may feel awkward, love demands that we draw a line of what is acceptable and unacceptable treatment. What does love look like? Love is doing what is best for the other person. Allowing another to treat us with blatant disregard and cruelty is unfair to both the giver and the receiver of such behavior. We owe it to our loved ones to say to them, "I love you too much to allow you to think it's all right to act so terribly."

No Rules? No Way!

Steve and I spend much of our time traveling to give concerts and sing at seminars. As a result we are required to eat out much of the time. When we're home in Tennessee, we would just as soon eat a sandwich in our own simple-but-clean kitchen than venture out to the fanciest of establishments. However, one evening we were dining at a nearby restaurant with some dear friends. I noticed that the advertising motto of this eatery was *"No Rules."* I'm sure the person responsible for this clever ad campaign probably worked on Madison Avenue and was paid a hefty six-figure salary for their ingenious suggestion. Perhaps they assumed, as a result of this carefree slogan, that patrons would be inspired to enjoy some sense of freedom and abandonment and maybe even order dessert.

As far as I was concerned, their intended response had exactly the opposite effect. Instead of the catchphrase making me feel free and easy, it actually made me feel uptight and uncomfortable, due to the fact that I feared their lackadaisical attitude may have found its way into the kitchen.

If I'm relaxing in a booth, waiting for my food to arrive, I want to know there are rules connected with my dining experience. For instance, I want the restaurant managers to have a hard-and-fast rule about food servers washing their hands after they visit the little girl's or boy's room. I want there to be an unbendable rule about what temperature foods must be stored at in the refrigerator. And how about an obliging rule forbidding mice droppings around the food preparation area? I can think of lots of rules that would make me feel safer and more comfortable as it pertains to my dining encounter. Having "no rules" does not make it "just right" in this consumer's humble opinion.

In the same way a standard of behavior in a commercial kitchen can make a patron feel free and relaxed as the meal is enjoyed, establishing and maintaining standards between family relationships can be just as liberating. In truth, boundaries are the best gift we can give ourselves. Without them we end up in big trouble. For instance, without boundaries in our physical life, we can end up unhealthy, overweight, and out-of-shape. When we live without guidelines in our spiritual life, we are loaded down with sin and the consequences of it. When we fail to set boundaries in our emotional lives, we (and others) end up falling prey to any thought that crosses our minds. Failing to take our thoughts captive to the obedience of Christ and failing to keep our hearts with all diligence leaves us open to having our "property lines" vulnerable to violation and trespassers.

What are some helpful guidelines that can help us live a more peaceful life when it comes to the challenge of living close to our families? The following are some boundaries families have found helpful. Recognizing that all relationships are different, and not all advice applies to every family, adopt any part of these "rules" that might help in your situation. Also, you don't have to live next door to one another for property lines to be crossed. Whether we live on the same street or several states away, we need clearly stated boundaries.

⊙ One mother-in-law who lived across the street from her daughter and her son-in-law said, "We never go to their house unless they call and invite us to come over. They know they are free to come to our house anytime. I just feel they need to have the assurance that we are not going to "drop in" for a surprise visit.

⊙ Even when we are invited, we call right before we come over. Any young wife enjoys the "two minute" warning that company is on the way.

⊙ There is a hard-and-fast rule that I follow. I never come into a house without knocking first. I learned this lesson from my mother-in-law. She had the most terrible habit of walking into our home unexpectedly and unannounced. One morning she came barging into the house, straight into our bedroom to tell me something. I was standing there completely naked. I was so irritated at her intrusion that I didn't even try to cover myself up with my hands or a towel. In all my glory I stood and looked her in the face as she delivered her "urgent" message. I think she finally got the point. She hasn't walked in without at least calling "yoo-hoo" since that revealing morning. I don't think either of us were ready for our relationship to move to that level.

⊙ No one loves their grandchildren more than me. I'm the obnoxious one at the party making everyone look at my "babies." However, it hurts me and sometimes it even makes me mad when my daughter-in-law assumes I will be the regular babysitter. Do I want to spend time with my grandchildren? You bet! Would I appreciate being asked with the option of saying no if I have other plans or if I simply don't feel like it that day? Absolutely! It's not just my daughter-in-law who does me that way. My daughter makes me feel guilty when I don't want to watch the children. She say things like, "I guess I'll just have to drop out of school if I can't depend on you to keep the kids." Am I the only person in the world capable of babysitting children? Give me a break!

⊙ My husband and I try to not call the children's house after the dinner hour. Of course, there have been emergency-type situations where we felt free to call, if needed. But we do not call just to talk when the family is supposed to be winding down for the day. It's been a while, but I remember what it's like to be bathing the baby and supervising homework and hearing the phone ring. I never want to be the one on the other end when our kids say, "Oh, no! Who's that calling at this hour?"

⊙ My son just started his own business. I know it takes time before the money starts to flow. We have offered him money in the past—actually we've insisted on giving it to him. Now, I'm beginning to see that we have been stepping over the boundaries. He wants to make it on his own, and we need to back off. From now on, we will only give him money if he asks for it. In our effort to make him feel loved and supported, I'm afraid we've made him feel less than the wonderful man he is.

⊙ I love it when my husband's parents come to visit, but to be honest, they stay too long. The old saying about fish and company stinking after three days applies here! Oh, yes! Someone needs to tell my in-laws. Unfortunately, my husband thinks it should be me who tells them. Personally, I'd rather they just read it in your book.

One Closing Thought

Some parents could give the best holiday gift this year to their adult children by having a family gathering without guilt. My husband, Steve, and I were blessed in that my mother and my mother-in-law worked together to coordinate the different meals and festivities. For instance, one mother would choose to have their main meal on Christmas Eve and the other one would choose Christmas Day. With them working out the details, it took the pressure off of us. Neither Steve nor I had to feel like we were disappointing our mothers.

Our children, on the other hand, have parents-in-law who live hundreds of miles away. Since both our children and their spouses live within 30 minutes from our house, I feel it is my place to release them to visit their in-laws on the actual holidays. In order to accommodate their traveling schedules, we've learned to celebrate *occasions* rather than *dates*. For example, we may have our Thanksgiving Dinner on Tuesday, rather than Thursday, and we are fine with that. Consequently, this system often leaves Steve and me alone on many holidays. But I'd rather be alone and satisfied with the holiday outcome than to be surrounded with tension!

In order to keep our children from feeling the "guilts" of us spending the holiday all alone, we often leave town and go visit Steve's parents or his sister, Jeannie. Somehow it makes it easier on our children if they think we are occupied. We are happy to do whatever it takes to help them feel the freedom to enjoy their other families.

From the time my son's wedding was being planned, I felt excluded. My feelings were given second-class attention. Nothing I wanted was acknowledged. This is my only son. How do I get over my hurt feelings and growing resentment? Every time I make progress at getting closer to my daughter-in-law, she pushes me away.

In my day, I was taught to respect my elders. I don't have a clue how to deal with this girl. Everything about her is the opposite of what I had hoped for in a daughter-in-law.

5

Waltzing to Rap Music

Time seems to pass us all like an unstoppable train. My elderly grandmother, who lived to be 93, put it all in a nutshell one day as she revealed how unmerciful the wildly spinning hands of the clock felt to her. Commenting on how the years seemed to pass in such an unfriendly way, she said, "I think time would fly even if I were in a penitentiary." Usually I think of the words of my wise grandmother on those days when the time between getting out of bed in the morning and getting back in it at night somehow seems like a blur. Mysteriously, it feels like one continuous motion. At the end of our days, Steve and I often comment, "Weren't we here just a few minutes ago?"

What is especially astounding about having seen a lot of miles is the way that age can bring a clearer view of life. The younger folks need the wisdom and caution of those who have ridden the time train such long distances. However, those whose engines are slowing would do well to remember that the youthful courage and boundless strength of the younger generation can be a source of fuel to their weary souls. The truth is, both the young and the old are passengers on the same train, and each group has incredibly valuable qualities that can be useful to the other. But there is an undeniable fact that cannot be ignored: Even though the train is barreling down the tracks, too often the cars are not connected. A dangerous gap exists between generations that needs to be addressed.

While there are many examples of the differences between the generations that exist, music is perhaps one of the most obvious. For some reason, each generation thinks the next one's taste in songs is abysmal. To illustrate, can any baby boomer forget the furor that was provoked when four shaggy-haired boys from Liverpool stepped off the plane and Beatlemania swept through the country in the early sixties? For some Sinatra-loving parents this invasion from England was nearly as unwelcomed at Hitler's march through France just 20 years earlier.

Looking back, it's almost humorous how some of the adults rose up in concert against the destructive influence of such lyrics as "I Wanna Hold Your Hand." Certainly, and sadly, that benign title is a long way from where we've come to. Parents now have to contend with such modern and explicit songs such as, "I Want to Sex You Up."

And it's not only secular music that can cause a rift between parent and child. Gospel music had a big influence on our parents' generation. Their hearts were moved to spiritual heights by the tight harmonies of the bouffant coiffures and matching-suit-wearing quartets of the forties and fifties. In contrast, by the time Steve and I were spiritually awakened, we were won over by the radical, blue-jeans-wearing, long-haired melodies of the folk-rock Christian music. Furthermore, just as our parents had not understood nor found it in their hearts to embrace all "that hippie, Jesus-freak music stuff," our children, in turn, stretched our musical tongues past their limit.

Just as our parents before us, we were honestly perplexed by what musically moved our kids to a place of worship in the seventies and eighties. It was really hard for us to enjoy the spandex-attired, make-up wearing, mullet-sporting men who were literally squatting and screaming the Scriptures. The sight of a group looking like the rock band Kiss on stage at a Christian music festival was not only hard on our eyes, but was tough to swallow. Steve and I have yet to understand the appeal of that music, and it is doubtful we ever will. Although we may struggle with such harmonic divisions, we have to face the fact that the "gap (not just the beat) goes on." As consolation, there's the irony of knowing that as "hip" and "with it" as our kids think they are, their children are going to regard them, someday, as "old fogies."

Bridging the Generation Gap Is a Family Affair

While the challenge of bridging the generational music gap may have been quite serious, it pales in comparison to the immense task of spanning the vast differences that exist between mothers-in-law and daughters-in-law. Keeping in mind that parents and their children may have had years in the home to work out the generational twists and turns that divide them, mothers-in-law and daughters-in-law are expected to be able to immediately accept one another and "dance" in beautiful rhythm even though they barely know one another. Some people even expect the two women to have their entire relationship worked out before the wedding reception has ended and the scattered rice is in the dust pan.

It takes time for the in-law two-step to be mastered. The dance is made difficult not only because the two women are virtual strangers, but because they are women of differing generations. What happens, for instance, when a young wife's desire to implement her own ideas and establish her own way

of doing things runs smack dab into the face of what her
mother-in-law might consider unacceptable? The gap widens
and the time train disconnects.

Spanning the Divide

I was a child of the fifties and a young woman in the sixties and seventies. Some of the things that my generation considered "far out" and downright radical for those times that
were rather appalling to my seniors don't seem so unusual in
this day and age. Such things as natural childbirth, breast
feeding, and working outside of the home took real intestinal
fortitude to do back then but are now pretty much accepted
as normal behavior.

Another example of where the gap was obvious between
the young and the old was in the area of education. It's not
unusual these days to hear that someone is homeschooling their
children. Today, in most circles, this mode of tutelage is socially
acceptable. However, the willingness to entertain alternative
styles of education has not always been met with such open-
mindedness.

When I started teaching Nathan at home in the early
eighties, I had to keep him inside during the break times for
fear that a neighbor might report him as being truant.
Thankfully, those days seem to be in the past. Now, there are
homeschool groups that regularly meet together to go on field
trips or participate in special activities. Some home educational
groups work with the local school systems, utilizing science
labs and athletic programs right alongside the public school
students.

Even though many individuals are more accepting of homeschooling as a vital, even preferred style of instruction, there

are still some who find little or no merit in this educational method. Those who object often perceive home education as an overreaction to the failures of the current school system. One mother-in-law, concerned for the well-being of her grandchildren, voiced her objection in this way: "Public school was good enough for my kids, and it should be good enough for my grandchildren. Why does my daughter-in-law think she can do a better job than trained professionals? I'm afraid my grandchildren are going to grow up and not be able to compete in college and the workplace. And how could they contend with those who have had more experience? They've been sheltered at home and not exposed to a real education and to the real world."

The trepidation on the part of the mother-in-law/grandmother is understandable. She should not be judged for her honest questioning of whether homeschooling is right for everyone. However, this woman from a generation passed needs to realize that times have changed; the cultural train has rolled on. The world her young daughter-in-law faces is not the same as in years past.

What a blessing this mother-in-law could be to her son's family if she would direct her concern in a more positive way. Offering to help with the younger children's education could prove a loving bridge to this generational divide. If she would consider leading field trips, starting baking classes, teaching sewing, or simply reading to her grandchildren, she could accomplish so much more than expressing her fears with curt words. Seeking to understand the differing viewpoints while constructively offering to assist can accomplish the goal of doing what is best for the next generation. Just think what an encouragement the mother-in-law could be if she would educate herself on the merits of homeschooling and, thus, become a support to her son's family rather than a stumbling block.

Understanding the Gap

Since we, the children of the sixties, rebelled against everything that got in our way, and since there was nothing left to mutiny against, you'd think the generation gap would have been bridged. However, we all know it still exists. As long as folks continue to live, there will be conflict between the differing ages. So the question remains, How radical must our adjustments be in order to accomplish the building of a bridge between the old and young? Perhaps not as drastic as the one I considered a few years ago.

As I have mentioned in my previous books, my mother and I shared a love of quilts. During her ten-year battle with cancer, she had a few months that were particularly difficult. My siblings and I took turns visiting and trying to help her and Dad as much as we could. During one of my visits Mom said, "I've always wanted an Amish quilt, but I guess I'm not going to live long enough to see one."

That's all she needed to say. The next day I was on the phone to my sweet friend from the Lancaster, Pennsylvania area. Linda and her husband, Nate, had sponsored Steve and me in a marriage retreat weekend at their Mennonite church. Since Linda had family who were Old Order Amish, I figured she might be able to help me find a quilt for my mother.

Plans were made for our trip, and Mom and Dad were all excited about their venture into Amish country. My daughter, Heidi, and I drove from Nashville to West Virginia. The next day we traveled to Pennsylvania. Just as I had imagined, Linda had planned the most unforgettable experience for us.

Along with gazing and drooling over some of the most beautiful quilts we had ever seen, one unexpected highlight of the trip was having supper at the home of Linda's Amish aunt. The food was unique and wonderfully delightful, but the cultural experience was different than anything we have ever had or since enjoyed.

As I was thinking about this subject of how the generations can relate to one another, my mind traveled back to that farmhouse in the lovely Pennsylvania countryside. It was the most impressive picture of how the generations can interact with one another. Granted, I was definitely seeing their situation from an outsider's romanticized viewpoint, but it seemed that the very young and the very old were living in a setting where each one was contributing to the productivity and the essential helpfulness required for the ongoing work and function of the farm and family.

I wondered why the generations seemed so able to live and love one another in this simple setting. Was the reason because of the lifestyle choice that had been made? As I observed their lives that seemed so unencumbered by technology, I had a radical thought. Perhaps the solution to the generation gap might be found in going outside and hacking down all the electrical poles in order to control the outside influences that seek to divide us as families. Maybe we should all quit our jobs, buy a farm, and return to a more agrarian culture.

Even though some who have been saturated by city life have actually tried and even been successful at selling their urban properties and buying a farm, these changes are not very likely to happen for most of us. In light of that truth, I have concluded that I must come to grips with the fact that other steps should be taken to span the generational differences. But in order to build the bridge, we need to know what the gap really is. What is it that older folks want that puts them at odds with the younger ones?

Generally speaking, the older generation seems prone to be more concerned with *how things look* and *what people think* about them. This is simply an observation of those who have lived long enough to know that "a good name is to be valued beyond rubies." They are biblically correct in that estimation. However, the temptation for those of older years is to spend their energy making things look right. Consequently, they can often lose sight of the need to be gracious in their quest for being right. Before those who are "seasoned passengers" on the time train jump off and throw this book away, let me say that this observation has its roots in the Scriptures.

Jesus did not hesitate to confront this generational problem in the book of Matthew, chapter 23. As you read it, you will see that He pronounces several judgments on the religious leaders of his day. The overemphasis they put on public pro-priety was contrasted with their lack of attention to private integrity. While the leaders were overly concerned with making sure everything looked good on the outside, the more impor-tant issues of honesty and proven character were painfully missing. Jesus effectively illustrated this lack in Matthew 23:25 with the example of washing the cup on the outside, while leaving the inside dirty and unusable.

I have personally felt the sting of this generational mis-emphasis in my college years.

When I was a student at Moody Bible Institute in the early seventies, a few of us undergraduates started a Bible study that would meet after our regular classes had ended for the day. There was a group of us who really longed to know God in a deeper, more intimate way. As we studied His Word and prayed together, we experienced a rich sense of His presence and His power.

For some strange reason, our study group became a threat of some sort to the administration of the school. One day someone reported us to the dean of students. We were all called into the office to give an account of our "nonconventional Bible study and behavior." What was our big sin? We were sitting on the floor during our Bible-study time. That conflict sounds so silly now (actually, it sounded ludicrous to us then), but keep in mind that this little battle took place during the "Jesus Movement" era. By sitting on the floor we "looked too radical" for the comfort level of those in authority. We had a generational disconnect that day. One of the students asked, "Isn't the position of our hearts before the Lord more important than the position of our bodies?" A good question indeed.

Though the "older generation" may have had a reason to be concerned, those of us who were on the floor had our own malfunctioning attitude that contributed to the division. For us, it was not just an appearance issue. It eventually became a matter of rebellion. While the older ones were concerned with looks, the younger folks were resistant to being controlled or told what to do. We were opposed to "the establishment."

The trouble that occurs, such as the one just described, between the generations can be avoided if both the young and the old will allow the Holy Spirit to be "the boss" in the situation. If the older generation refuses to yield to the Lord, then a prideful "it's my way or the highway" attitude will prevail. However, just as the older ones should be careful in how they approach the conflict, the younger ones also need to carefully guard their choice of lyrics as they sing their songs of independence. If the younger ones do not submit their ways to the Lord, then rebellion and anger can result.

Ultimately, the generation gap seems to be a battle between pride and rebellion. Is it any wonder there are so many causalities in this war? The answer to the conflict is for each person to allow God to place in him or her a gentle heart free from judgment. Both the old and the young are to learn from each other. While understanding that the answer to an aging pride is humility, the answer to youthful rebellion is a teachable spirit.

Bridging the Gap with Wisdom

In an effort to carefully side with the virtues of wisdom gained by riding the time train a long way down the tracks, may I say to the young women that undoubtedly there are those older ones who genuinely care about youthful co-passengers. They have the wisdom that helps them recognize dangers that may turn out to be a terrible mistake or lack of judgment on the younger person's part. A mother-in-law shared with me her account of how seasoned wisdom unintentionally collided with a youthful plan.

A few days after her granddaughter was born, Mary and her husband, John, excitedly packed up the car to make the seven-hour trip to see the sweet baby girl. During the visit, she learned that the young mother had been reading literature on how to properly care for her new baby. Her daughter-in-law was an intelligent, well-read young woman who prided herself on investigating the facts before she would commit herself to a plan. After learning as much as she could about the subject of child-nourishment, she became convinced that breast-feeding would be the best means of feeding her newborn.

The mother-in-law was from a different time and era. None of her family members or friends had chosen to breast-feed their infants, yet she realized that this was not her decision. The mother-in-law was determined to hold her tongue.

The in-laws were there for a few hours, and the mother-in-law noticed that the baby was always whimpering, if not outright crying. There seemed be something wrong with the baby. The grandmother was concerned at the baby's lack of well-being, but was relieved when she realized that the infant was due for her doctor's appointment later in the afternoon.

When they took the baby to the doctor, it was revealed that the baby was not gaining weight the way that she should. The doctor questioned the mother, inquiring how the breast-feeding experience was going. Even though the child nursed almost constantly, evidently she was not getting the nourishment she needed from her mother's milk.

The mother-in-law assumed that the doctor's evaluation would put an end to the breast-feeding experiment. But that was not to be the case. A generational conflict was starting to brew between the two women. Regardless of the seeming lack of success with the breast-feeding, the young mother insisted on continuing to nurse her baby. All the information in the literature confirmed that if she kept nursing, her milk would eventually come in.

However, the mother-in-law was not about to sit around and let her grandchild go hungry. Whether it was right or wrong to interfere, when the daughter-in-law left to go to the store, the mother-in-law found a baby bottle and some formula and fed the baby some milk. Fully satisfied, the baby stopped crying and went fast asleep.

Could this situation have been resolved without the mother-in-law becoming involved? The mother-in-law said, "Since my daughter-in-law wouldn't listen to the doctor, I didn't think I had much of a chance of getting through to her. This predicament was not about me winning, nor was it about my daughter-in-law proving her point. An innocent child was suffering, and I needed to do what I could to alleviate the problem."

When the mother-in-law confessed her breach of nursing etiquette to her daughter-in-law, some choice words were exchanged between the two of them. Eventually, however, they both were able to agree on the real issue. The baby was more important than her mother's plan or her grandmother's opinion. The solution that was reached resulted in a happy, healthy baby. She was lovingly nursed at her mother's breast and also given an occasional bottle, just to top off her additional need for nourishment.

You may recall in an earlier chapter, I suggested that the appropriate response to an adult/children scenario is "sure," "wow," or "really." Even though the story just related may seem contradictory to that advice, I still stand by that recommendation. When the only ones who might get hurt are the adults, then in that case the in-laws should seriously limit their involvement. But everything changes when the health and safety of an innocent child is at stake. There are situations that warrant a grandparent taking the risk of "getting in trouble" with adult children in order to protect a minor.

Bridging the Gap with Knowledge

One daughter-in-law, who had been married for several years and was a mother of three children, came up to the edge of the generation gap and tumbled right into it. Actually, her husband pushed her into it, but in her mind, fair or not, she held her mother-in-law responsible. The problem began many years earlier. Her hubby had been raised by a doting mother who did everything for her family. She required nothing from her husband or sons when it came to helping with the work around the house.

Since this woman's mother-in-law was able to "do it all," the son grew up assuming his future wife would be able to do the same. When his idea of a perfect home situation didn't look identical to his parents' arrangement, he felt disappointed and confused. Why should he have to help with dinner or wash the dishes? Why did his wife expect him to run the vacuum cleaner when he came home from working all day?

This man had never seen his dad lift a helping finger around the house. Yet, the house was always clean and every night when the dad came home from work, a home-cooked meal was ready on the table as soon as he walked through the door. The husband had always envisioned and secretly longed for the same kind of care afforded his father. He had been bitterly perturbed that his wife was incapable or, worse than that, unwilling to do what his mother's generation had made look so effortless.

In the midst of his disappointment he failed to acknowledge that there was one huge difference between the life his mother lived and that of his wife's. The latter worked over 40 hours a week outside the home. Not only did she carry out a full-time job that required many hours at the office, sometimes she worked at home well into the evening. She was swamped at her job, but she was also responsible for their three children's constant need of transportation to and from their multitude of extracurricular activities.

With her full-time employment, managing the needs of the home, and taking care of the children, she was a woman stressed to the max and tired to the bone. Her husband's desire to replicate his father's world, made possible by a "supermom," had forgotten to factor in the additional demands on his wife's time and energy. Yes, his mother was always home when he arrived from school. Since there was no second car she didn't spend endless hours driving countless miles carpooling and chauffeuring the children around town.

Finally, the exhausted and exasperated wife sat down with her bewildered husband and in a nonemotional, yet honest moment explained to him how much it hurt her to be expected to do the impossible. "If I'm going to work outside of the home, then you're going to have to pitch in and help me at home. I can't do everything your mother did if I'm going to work a job."

By being such a "do everything" woman, this man's mother put her son at a distinct disadvantage and left the daughter-in-law to fill unwearable shoes. He had never had to pick up after himself or do his own laundry, consequently his wife was put into a most uncomfortable position. Since his mother had not done it, his wife had to teach him how to help around the home. Neither the wife, nor her husband were very happy with the situation, but it couldn't be avoided. Even though the mother-in-law may have assumed she was being a superior mother by not requiring anything from her children, in this modern day when it is not uncommon for both men and women to share the bread-winning position, she failed to equip her son for a different generational experience. My intention is not to be critical of this mother-in-law. I'm sure she did what she thought was right and good for her family. But it was unreasonable to expect his young wife who works outside of the home to maintain the same standard of housekeeping as his mother who was home all day.

Unmothered...Unmentored

Not only do some men seem to be clueless on how to keep house, but many of the young women of the present generation haven't the foggiest notion of how to effectively and efficiently manage a home either. What once was a priority in the minds of many mothers and grandmothers, teaching the young women how to take care of a family, has been sorely neglected in favor of other career choices. When I wrote *Ten Things I Want My Daughter to Know*, I did so with the conviction that my age group of women has produced the most unmothered, unmentored group of young ladies of any generation. We must now mend what has been broken through our neglect and help these young women prepare to care for their families.

When I was a young lady, there were several different ways in which we received our instruction on caring for a home. Not only was the older generation careful to educate us, but schools offered classes in home economics. As I understand now, however, the curriculum in many of the schools has been adapted toward a more gender inclusive approach. Thus, the schools that once taught young girls how to sew and cook basic foods are putting their resources into such programs as career development and financial investment courses. While these may be worthy studies, they don't do much toward teaching a young lady (or young man!) how to prepare a meal, administer first aid, or sew a ripped seam.

The Generational Dance

One of the most memorable moments I can recall was at the stroke of midnight at the turn of the millennium. Our son, Nathan, had promised his Grandmother Chapman many years earlier that when the bell was tolling in the year 2000, the two of them would dance in the street in celebration of the coming of the twenty-first century. They did just that, and we have the pictures to prove it.

Their dance was a vivid portrait of what has been addressed in this chapter. Nathan's youthful, strong legs inspired his 70-something grandmother to dance a little faster. At the same time, desiring to protect her fragile back, his dance steps slowed down a bit. By meeting in the middle, their movements were graceful, successful, and unforgettable.

The same can be true for energetic young wives and experienced mothers-in-law. When each one yields to the needs of the other, they can get along as they dance across the generation gap. God's Word reminds us that we each have a part to play that meshes together:

> It will come about after this that I will pour out My Spirit on *all* mankind; and your sons and daughters will prophesy, your *old* men will dream dreams, your *young* men will see visions.

When I met my husband we were students in college. I was from New Jersey, and he was from Mississippi. I found his Southern manners and country drawl absolutely irresistible. He thought I was fascinating—different than any girl he'd ever met. I was more talkative and demonstrative than the other young ladies he had dated from back home. My take-charge attitude and bold ambition captured his heart. Everything was great until he took me home to meet his folks.

From the beginning of our visit I was a little taken aback. I had not planned on a reenactment of the Civil War. Since I was from "up there," they immediately tagged me a "Yankee." My open, loud, opionionated ways were appalling to them.

When I first met his mother, I did what I would have done if I were greeting my own mother. I wrapped my arms around her and gave her a big hug and kiss. Her nonresponse was surprising and rather hurtful. Hugging her was like embracing a dead fish. Now, 25 years later, my in-laws love me and think I'm incredible. And I'm happy to say, the feeling is mutual. However, that transformation from leery to loving didn't happen overnight—nor did it happen by mistake. There was some real effort put forth on both sides of the Mason–Dixon Line to bring this Yankee and those Southerners together. I am thrilled to say that my mother-in-law and I are now best of friends. Who would have ever thought it could be this way?

6

Square Dancing
on a Round Floor

Anyone who's been married any length of time knows that there are as many challenges to a successful marriage as there are fish in the sea. Even for those individuals who come from very similar family structures, the most insignificant difference can easily become an issue for fiery debate. For instance, one young wife expressed her surprise at what an adjustment it was spending the holidays with her in-laws.

Anna came from a rather large family that enjoyed the hustle and bustle of the Christmas experience. She said,

> In my family, we always got up at first light on Christmas morning. The early-risers would go and roust out of bed all the sleepyheads. We then would run downstairs to the living room. With Mom and Dad sitting in their pajamas on the couch, watching with amusement, the kids would begin opening the gifts. The room was filled with squeals of delight. Hugs and thank yous rang out from every corner of the room.

Even though Anna married a man whose family was very similar socially, economically, and culturally, she was not prepared for the vast difference in how they did things. She contrasted the exuberance of her own family's traditions with that of her husband's:

> It was quite a shock the first Christmas morning at my in-laws. Eventually, everyone got up and leisurely meandered into the living room. They sat around the Christmas tree, drinking coffee, talking, and munching on Christmas cookies. I kept waiting for the stampede toward the mountain of gifts located within arm's reach. But to my amazement, no one made a move toward the colorfully wrapped bounty under the Christmas tree. I asked what I considered to be a logical question: "When do we open the gifts?" They looked at me like I had crabs crawling out my ears.
>
> My husband informed me in a rather hushed whisper, "We don't open gifts until after dinner." What? Who ever heard of going all Christmas Day without opening your gifts? At that moment I sincerely wondered, "What kind of nuthouse did I marry into?"

If the relatively unimportant issue of when we open the Christmas gifts can be the cause of division and consternation in a family, consider how significant a challenge it could be when a husband and wife arrive at the altar from totally different cultural experiences. Here's what one wife shared about her situation.

> From the very beginning of our marriage, I felt like everyone was watching me. Even though my husband loved and accepted me, I was very much aware that socially we came from two different worlds. I voiced my concerns about the societal divide, but my husband dismissed them as irrelevant. He felt that love was all

that mattered, and that our Christian commitment to the Lord and to one another was strong enough to overcome any superficial differences that might exist.

Now, after being married a while, I'm not sure those variances were so insignificant. To illustrate what kind of adjustments were necessary, consider how we were raised. I was brought up in a tiny little house out in the country located on a small farm. Believe it or not, until I was in junior high, we didn't even have indoor plumbing. Although my parents were financially poor, they were wonderfully decent, kind, and godly people. In contrast to how I was raised, my husband came from a wealthy family who lived in a beautiful mansion. He never had to work for his money, and he had servants who tended to his every need. His father was an important businessman and civic leader in the community. Everyone knew them and expected my husband to follow his father's very successful footsteps.

A few months after we got married, we moved back to his hometown. Living there was like taking up residence in a fishbowl. Every time I bought a new dress or tried a new hairdo, everyone knew it before I got home. Oddly enough, news of such insignificant events traveled the grapevine faster than an Elvis sighting.

Although my mother-in-law was very kind to me, my own insecurity and lack of confidence caused me to feel judged for my lack of social skills. I was uncomfortable around my husband's family because I was afraid I would be blamed if he, the heir apparent to the family business, didn't succeed to their expectations. I'm not sure my husband and I realized how difficult it would be to merge two lives from such different social levels.

Appreciation

Bridging the gap between the social, economical, and cultural divides that exist when two families are united is never easy, but it is possible. One daughter-in-law, who had been raised in a very affluent home, shared with me how she sought to span the gap between her world and the one in which her mother-in-law lived.

> From the moment I met my mother-in-law, I could tell she was suspicious of me. I couldn't blame her for wondering if I was capable of being a good wife to her son. The truth be known, I had never worked a day in my life. I saw no need to pick up after myself because there was always someone else there to do it for me. I never had to worry about money, it was just always there. I couldn't cook, and I didn't know the first thing about taking care of a husband or a house.
>
> In contrast, my mother-in-law had worked nonstop all her life. Her husband had left her to raise their six children all alone when the youngest was just a baby. She worked the night shift and then came home to tend the farm during the day. Growing their own food was the only way her family could survive. To say that my mother-in-law and I came from different worlds is a gigantic understatement.

Longing to be included as a part of my husband's family, I realized early on that if the differences between us were going to be bridged, I was going to have to come her way. She could not come to my world, but I could go to hers. Each time my husband and I would visit my mother-in-law, I made a conscious effort to learn something from her. Not only was I an eager student, but she was a patient teacher. In fact, she's the one who taught me to cook, to grow a garden, and to preserve the produce through the process of canning. Once she realized that I didn't look down on her for the circumstances of her life but truly appreciated and admired all that she had accomplished, our relationship started to change.

Every individual longs to be appreciated and acknowledged for what he or she has done. Mothers-in-law and daughters-in-law are no different. The relationship between the female in-laws can be greatly enhanced when both of them are careful to express that mutual appreciation.

One way a daughter-in-law can bridge what may appear as miles of empty expanse is with simple words of gratitude. The following proclamation is the expression of my heart toward the mother-in-law who lovingly raised my husband.

Dear Mother-in-Law,
Thank you for being such a wonderful mother
to your son, my husband.
It is because of your hard work that I am blessed
to be married to the most wonderful man alive.

You share experiences with him, as his mother,
that I can never fully comprehend.
It was you who ran to his side
and comforted him
in the middle of the night
when a bad dream interrupted
his peaceful slumber.
Holding back your tears so he wouldn't see you cry,
you're the one who drove
him to the hospital when he
fell off the bike and broke his arm.
It was at his bedside that you knelt and
prayed
with him each night and
shared God's Word
with him each morning before
he ran off to school.
You helped him with his science projects,
sewed his Pilgrim's costume
for the Thanksgiving Day pageant,
and nursed him back to health
when he had the measles.
For every act of kindness you did,
for every character-building word
you shared with him,
I am indebted to you.

Appreciation is a bridge with two lanes. Just as daughters-in-law need to express words of appreciation, mothers-in-law can offer the same courtesy to their daughters-in-law in words such as these:

Dear Daughter-in-Law,
Thank you for loving my son.

Because you are in his life,
I have seen a side of him emerge
that is more loving
and more kind than before he met you.
I am tremendously grateful to you
for investing your time and energy in my son,
although I believe him to be worthy of that investment.
Thank you for feeding him
and caring for his every need.
Thank you for adjusting your life,
adapting your ways,
and for those times when you
basically put up with him
when he acts more like a little boy
than the noble man he really is.
If I had been given the chance,
I couldn't have picked anyone
more wonderful or more suitable
for him than you.
Thank you for being
a haven of rest for his soul
and for being that lovely
"soft place for him to land."
I'm filled with gratitude toward you
for sharing his future with him.
And last, but certainly not least,
thank you for allowing your body
to be used as a loving home
to grow your children.
I am indebted to you.

Acceptance

Along with expressing words of appreciation and admira-
tion for what the mother-in-law and the daughter-in-law have

done, it is essential for each person to accept the God-given position the other holds in the family.

How does the daughter-in-law relate to the spiritual position given to the mother-in-law? Just as the son is instructed to *honor* and *respect* his parents, it is equally important for the daughter-in-law to do the same. (And, of course, the husband is to treat his wife's parents with equal respect.)

When God presented Moses with the Ten Commandments, the fifth one—and the very first command that involved human/family relations—is the one in which we are instructed to honor our parents. This commandment is also referenced in Matthew 15:3-7. Jesus was asked by the religious leaders why He allowed His disciples to ignore the tradition of washing their hands before they ate. Jesus responded, "And why do your traditions violate the direct commandments of God? For instance, God's law is 'Honor your father and mother; anyone who reviles his parents must die.' But you say, 'Even if your parents are in need, you may give their support money to the church instead.' And so, by your man-made rule, you nullify the direct command of God to honor and care for your parents. You hypocrites!" (TLB).

The words of Jesus leave no doubt that honoring our parents is a command that is required by God's decree and an act that love demands. It is as vital and relevant now as it was in the Old Testament times.

Not only are we to honor our mothers-in-law even as we should honor our own mothers, but there is an additional responsibility if both the mother-in-law and the daughter-in-law are Christians. In Titus 2, younger women are to show respect and honor for the older women in the church. When we fully embrace the scriptural mandate of respecting and honoring our mothers-in-law, we are truly building a bridge across the chasm of our differences.

The Wife Trumps Mother Every Time

There is no doubt, according to the Word of God, that the position of the wife is a superior role when it comes to the marriage union. Ephesians 5:31 quotes a passage from the book of Genesis when it says, "For this reason a man shall *leave* his father and *mother* and shall be joined to his *wife,* and the two shall become one flesh" (emphasis added). To put it as simply and understandably as possible, that passage means: *"Sonny is to leave his mommy and cleave to his honey."*

I realize it may be difficult to swallow this admonition, and I understand the struggle. I, too, am a loving mother to my son. And it is because of that immense love that I beseech you to let go. Stop interjecting yourself into the affairs of your son, and allow him to embrace the wife of his youth. By living in obedience to God's Word, you open the door of blessing on your life, but you are also creating an environment where your son and his new family can enjoy a happy, healthy relationship with you.

Affection

I once heard it said, "Everyone is normal, until you get to know them." That statement could not be more true than when it comes to families. Even those folks who seemingly share similarities in all areas, including socially, financially, and culturally, if you scratch beneath the surface, you undoubtedly find more differences than commonalities. And that's just fine. Just because our families are not alike and may do things differently doesn't mean one is right and the other is wrong. Like spices in a chili recipe that gives it its unique taste, our idiosyncrasies keep things interesting and free of boredom.

When a mother-in-law and a daughter-in-law learn to express appreciation and acceptance for one another—despite the differences that may exist—the end result is a *bridge built by love.* No matter what time and stress may do to the structure, when love is the binding material, the span cannot be destroyed.

One mother-in-law who has practiced the power of love wrote to me and said, "We refer to our 'in-laws' as our 'in-loves' because we gained two more members of our family by them being 'in love' with our born children." I like that! Keep in mind that love is an *act of the will,* not a result of emotions. When love flows from treating one another kindly, then it only gets stronger and sweeter over time.

Some daughters-in-law shared a few special remembrances about the mothers-in-law they love. I am inspired by these comments and have as my hope that some of these sweet observations will be said of me someday.

I appreciate my mother-in-law because...

- ⊙ she doesn't meddle in our affairs.

- ⊙ she's like a second mother to me. My mom lives so far away, it's nice to have someone who loves and cares for me.

- ⊙ she's an example of gentleness. She was such a big help when our babies were born. I felt unsure of myself, but she kept telling me that I was a good mother.

- ⊙ I had a bad relationship with my own mother, but my mother-in-law treated me so kindly that it helped heal the wounds from my past.

⊙ she always said wonderful, complimentary things about me to her son. That made me proud, and I think helped my husband treat me better.

⊙ when I married my husband, I brought with me a child from a previous marriage. My mother-in-law didn't treat my daughter any differently than she did her other grandchildren. Being loving to my child was the most wonderful thing my mother-in-law could ever have done for me. As far as I'm concerned, she can do no wrong!

⊙ whenever she bought her daughter a gift, she would get me something, too. It made me feel as though she loved me as a daughter. I cared about the gift, but it was her including me that blessed me the most.

Repairing Your Relationship

What do we do if we've done it all wrong? Can the societal bridge be repaired if by our own hands and tongues we have ripped out the floor and now have no place to dance? There is hope and healing for relationships if we humble ourselves, admit our part in the destruction of the bridge, and willingly offer and accept the forgiveness of one another. One young daughter-in-law regretfully said,

> I wish I had done things differently in the beginning of my relationship with my mother-in-law. When my husband and I were dating, I told him that I didn't think he should be living with his parents. As we got more and more serious about one another, I informed him that if he didn't move out of his mother's house immediately, then I wouldn't marry him. Today, I

question my actions and demands. Even though I still believe it was a good thing for him to live on his own for a while, I now realize that I was out of line to give him such an ultimatum without taking into account his mother's feelings. I think she saw me as a threat to her relationship with her son, and I suppose she was right. I should not have interjected myself into the situation by insisting that he choose my wants over the needs of his mother.

Looking back, I see that I was trying to rip him away from his mom. Instead, I should have taken it a little slower and recognized that her son getting married and moving away was difficult on her. I know I owe her an overdue apology.

My hope and prayer is that when this daughter-in-law asks her mother-in-law to forgive her, forgiveness will be graciously extended. If not, the result will be as described in a quote from Thomas Fuller: "He that cannot forgive others breaks the bridge over which he must pass himself; for every man has need to be forgiven." Matthew 5:7 says it this way, "Blessed are the merciful, for they shall receive mercy."

The original meaning of the word "mercy" indicates that exercising this toward another is not simply experiencing a thought or feeling. The emotion felt is meant to *provoke us to an action*. What is the appropriate reaction to showing mercy to another? Forgiving them. When we are willing to show mercy by offering and accepting forgiveness for things done in ignorance, or even with malice, then when we have need of mercy, the Bible tells us that we will receive it.

As we allow our hearts to be tenderized by God's love, we will find the strength to apply the healing balm of appreciation and the salve of acceptance toward those who have been brought into our lives by love and law. Even when our families are different and, consequently, do things differently, as mothers-in-law and daughters-in-law we can learn from each other and build that bridge of love that can connect social, financial, and cultural divides. May we all not be satisfied to live our lives void of loving relationships with our in-laws. And may we do all that is within our power to make sure we are not the stumbling block to a healthy relationship. May our goal be as high as that of the great missionary and martyr Jim Elliott: "In my life I do not want to be a milestone that people pass by and remember. I want to be a fork in the road that because of the clarity of my life men choose one way or the next."

I've never given my mother-in-law a reason to distrust me. For 40 years I have been a faithful, loving wife, serving my husband almost to a fault. (Okay, I've spoiled him rotten!) I've always been there for my children and now for my grandchildren. What can I do to make my mother-in-law trust me? She spies on me (yes, she lives in the same neighborhood) and talks about me to relatives behind my back. And, at times, she is openly hostile toward me. Nonetheless, when she's sick I'm the one who takes food to her. When she needs to go to the doctor, I'm the one who takes her to her appointment. It's not fair that I'm treated so poorly. Yet, when my friends tell me to leave her alone and let her fend for herself, I feel sorry for her. As a Christian, am I obligated to help her even when she's so mean to me?

7

When You Hear a Different Beat

One definition of the word "fellowship" is of two fellows in a ship going to the same destination. With that meaning in mind, if a mother-in-law and daughter-in-law are to enjoy a true sense of fellowship, it is essential for them to be going in the same direction. This truth is never more applicable than in the area of shared religious faith.

What does a mother-in-law or daughter-in-law do when that shared faith is not only absent but may even be found to be a stumbling block and a point of contention between them? How does the other respond when her faith in Christ becomes a source of hostility in the relationship?

One daughter-in-law who had been married for 35 years, told of the struggle she experienced in trying to share the love of Christ with her husband's mother. She wrote,

> My mother-in-law invited me to her home a few days after my marriage to her son. Since the courtship to my husband had been rather brief, I was looking forward to the opportunity to get to know her and the rest of the family better. Being a believer in Jesus and wanting to share the good news of what He had done in my life, I was very open about my faith. Finally I found an opportunity to do so, and I excitedly seized it. I was honestly taken aback by her quick response

to my zealous witness of Christ. She wheeled around on her heels, faced me squarely, and with a very stern voice, she said, "I have read the Bible many times, and I don't want you to ever tell me anything about Jesus."

I'm embarrassed to admit it, but as a young 21-year-old bride, I shrank back and never mentioned anything again to her about the Lord. I've never felt such a burden of heart as I did at her funeral. Since that day, I've thought about all the times I could have shared the gospel with her. Even though I tried to live my life in such a way as to demonstrate the love of God, I still have regrets because I'm not sure she ever made peace and received Christ as her Savior.

It's not only daughters-in-law who have been frustrated in giving a witness of Christ. A mother-in-law shared how she tried to no avail to win her daughter-in-law to the Lord.

When my son married his wife, I liked her enough, but I was very concerned that he was marrying a nonbeliever. My son has been raised in the church since he was born. I warned him about dating women who did not share his faith. He always said that I was overreacting and would reassure me when they dated, "We're just going out to eat, Mom. We're not going to run off and get married."

Since the wedding I have constantly prayed for this young lady. She is not open to the gospel at all. Sadly, today my son doesn't get up on Sunday morning and go to church anymore. I can see him slipping into attitudes and behaviors I never thought I would ever see.

I have tried to talk to her, but it only pushes her farther away. My only recourse is prayer.

Giving or Being a Witness for Christ

Whether you're a mother-in-law or a daughter-in-law who is hopeful that you can offer an effective witness of your faith in Christ, keep in mind that *giving* a witness can be different than *being* a witness. I remember an old poem from years ago that says,

> I'd rather see a sermon
> Than hear one any day
> I'd rather one would walk with me
> Than merely tell the way
> The eye's a better pupil
> And more willing than the ear
> Fine counsel is confusing
> But example's always clear[1]

If your in-law seems to be open to your message of the Good News of Jesus Christ, I encourage you to tread carefully on the sacred ground of her seeking heart. I urge you to do so because of the eternal impact your witness may have on her life. Beating her with spiritual rules and regulations will likely not accomplish the goal. To illustrate a wrong approach, I take you back to 1967 to the halls of my alma mater.

When I was in high school, I was a very religious person. In fact, my senior year I received a 25-dollar award for being "the most religious." One day following the award ceremony, a fellow classmate came to me as I was getting my books out of my locker. At his young age, he was seeking truth and to my regret I inadvertently misled him. He said to me, "What do I have to do to be saved?" As a person who desired to be an active witness for Christ, his words were what I longed to hear.

While his question was excellent, my answer was less than helpful. I didn't share with him that Jesus loved him and had already done all that was required of him to receive eternal life. I didn't share with him that salvation was a free gift, and we couldn't do anything to earn it. No, I addressed his earnest inquiry with, "Do you smoke? Then stop smoking. Do you drink? Stop drinking. Do you go to church on Sundays? Quit your Sunday morning job and start attending services. Stop cussing and read your Bible and pray."

It was not until several years later that I came to understand that it was not by a person's good works, but by the completed work of Christ on the cross that a joyful walk with Him can be experienced. Titus 3:5-6 NIV tells us: "He saved us, not because of righteous things we had done, but because of His mercy. He saved us through the washing of rebirth and renewal by the Holy Spirit."

The freedom I experienced when I traded Satan's lie for the truth is indescribable. However, it was not too long after I came to such a peaceful revelation that I remembered my response to my young friend's question in high school. I prayed for a second chance to set the record straight. That opportunity came at our ten-year high school reunion.

As I joined my classmates who gathered that day at the city park, I sought out my misguided friend. I found him sitting with his family. Eagerly, I began to sincerely apologize for misleading him on that day he had asked me "the question." Earnestly, I shared with him the hope and peace I had found in a relationship with Jesus. However, his response to my belated, corrected sermon was not what I had hoped.

Sadly enough, he very quickly excused himself and wandered off into the crowd. I realized that the truth I had so longed to bring to him had not captured his interest. To be honest, there was a sense of self-blame that pricked my heart. Yet all I could do was pray that although I had not given him the "right answer" that day so long ago, God was not limited by my lack of knowledge. I do believe that if my friend was really a seeker, God would override my honest, but sincerely wrong attempt at evangelism.

Are you attempting to make attractive a life of following Christ? Please keep in mind that the whip of laws will wound, but the soft hands of love will heal. Thankfully, the very best example of hands that can lead a soul to a life-giving faith are the nail-scarred hands of Christ Himself. He can show us what to do to witness to our loved ones.

What Did Jesus Do?

Media such as bracelets, headbands, ball caps, and T-shirts advertise the popular question "WWJD?" (What would Jesus do?) In the case of what methods a person can use to deliver the love of God to another, it might be helpful to ask, instead, "What *did* Jesus do?" His actions and reactions are sufficiently recorded for us in the Scriptures. And for the sake of this discussion concerning how mothers-in-law and daughters-in-law can bridge the spiritual gap, what Jesus did as He interacted with the women of His day can be priceless information.

Some may ask, "What possible relevance could it be to our present-day existence how Jesus treated women 2000 years ago?" The answer to this very good question could yield the results that a mother- or daughter-in-law need. To search out the answer, let's first go to Hebrews 13:8. It is perhaps one of the most important verses in the entire Bible: *"Jesus is the same yesterday, today and yes, forever"* (emphasis added).

This particular passage indicates why Christianity is so different than any other religion, and why those who long to share the life of Christ can be so motivated to do so. There are Muslims, Hindus, Buddhists, Jews, and folk from many other religious persuasions who believe that Jesus *was* a good man. They believe that He *was* responsible for performing miracles and feeding the multitudes. They say He *was* a great teacher. Some will even go so far as to admit that He *was* a prophet, a holy man. As factual as all these things are, the truth that sets Christianity apart from all the other world religions is that we believe that our Savior *is still* the same today as He was then. Believing this to be true, it is understandable that many Christian in-laws feel deeply passionate about their message of the hope found in Jesus Christ and would want to "win" their loved ones over to His mercy and grace.

Jesus—A Friend to Sinners

If in-laws want to heal a relationship by *being* a witness of "what Christ did," displaying a forgiving spirit is probably the best place to start. For a beautiful example of the merciful act of the Lord's forgiveness we can look in the Gospel of John, chapter 8. Many of us are familiar with the account of the woman who was found committing adultery. She was brought to Jesus by the religious leaders and thrown into the dirt at His feet. These scholars of the religious Law then proceeded to set before Jesus a serious dilemma.

"Teacher, this woman has been caught in adultery, in the very act. Now in the Law Moses commanded us to stone such women; what then do You say?"

Of course, this situation was not really about the woman. The purpose for this drama was an attempt by the angry religious leaders of His day to catch Jesus in a snare. Jesus knew that if He said, "Yes, the Law requires this woman to die. Go ahead and stone her," then He would have proven Himself to be a hypocrite. The religious vanguard knew that Jesus was known to be merciful to sinners. Perhaps they thought if He sided with them, then He would have lost the good will of the common person.

On the other hand, if Jesus said, "No, do not kill her," He knew He would have put Himself at odds with the Law of Moses. In the deviant minds of those who brought the woman to Jesus, it was a win–win situation for them. Either one of these responses would do the trick of tripping Him up.

Much to their frustration, Jesus wisely gave neither of the answers the religious men expected. First of all, Mosaic Law does not say only she is to be killed. The Law demanded both the man and woman be punished. If she was caught in the very act of adultery, it shouldn't have been too difficult for her accusers to determine who the fellow was that was doing the deed with her.

Jesus stooped down in the dirt, positioning Himself beside the pitiful woman. If we had been observing from a distance, perhaps we might have mistakenly assumed Jesus was the one with whom she had sinned. He who knew no sin was not threatened to identify with the sinner. Then in an act of divine genius, Jesus turned His attention from the woman and began to write on the ground with His finger. For generations people have speculated about what Jesus may have been writing. Perhaps He was writing down the names of the folks in the crowd and listing their sins. Or maybe He was documenting the names of those in the crowd who had also partaken of her favors. The possibilities go on and on. One thing is for sure, when He looked up at the crowd and made His next statement, everything changed.

He said to those with the rocks in their hands, "He who is without sin among you, let him be the first to throw a stone at her." And He once again turned His attention to what He was writing on the ground.

Can you imagine how it must have felt to be the woman who was helplessly lying in the dirt, waiting for the impact of the first stone to crash against her body. Huddled on the ground, did she contemplate the life choices that had brought her to such a sad state? Did she remain silent, determined if she hadn't been able to live with dignity that at least she wouldn't give her accusers the satisfaction of hearing her cry out and plead for mercy. Though we don't know what she might have been thinking, one question we can surely ask is, What did she think when she first heard the sound of stones hitting the ground and the shuffling of her accusers feet as they were backing away. In the deafening silence, she must have slowly looked up to find only one person standing there. As Jesus stood up and wiped the dust from the fleshly pen of His finger, He diverted His attention from His writing and directed His words to the pitiful adulteress in the dirt.

"Woman, where are they? Did no one condemn you?" She replied to Jesus' inquiry, "No one, Lord." Jesus then said the words of hope that have echoed throughout all of the ages in guilty hearts: "I do not condemn you, either. Go. From now on sin no more."

What? No lecture? No "you got by with it this time, but if there's a next time, you're on your own"? Did Jesus not care that she had sinned? Of course He cared. No one knew more than Jesus how sin destroys the sinner. But His mercy and love were bigger than her sin...and they are bigger than ours, too.

Jesus—A Friend to the Nameless

A daughter-in-law told me a story I found quite humorous. She said,

> For the first eight years of my marriage, I didn't know what to call my mother-in-law. Calling her "mom" was totally out of the question. I already had a perfectly wonderful mother, so that handle was not appropriate. It felt much too formal to call her by her full name, Mrs. _____. And I was equally uncomfortable calling her by her first name. That seemed too informal. I finally resorted to never addressing her directly. My husband thought it was hysterical that I allowed something to tie me up so tightly. He would mischievously enjoy watching me as I sat quietly waiting until I could catch her eye. When she would look at me, I would then ask her whatever I needed to. Needless to say, family gatherings were very awkward for me.

Whether we choose to call our in-laws "mom" or "dad" or stick to using their legal names is really one of the lesser decisions we must make in life. But as mothers-in-law and daughters-in-law who are seeking to cultivate an enjoyable relationship with the other, we should keep in mind that names have tremendous impact.

When I was a child, I was called my share of hurtful, nasty names. And I must admit that I called others equally bad ones. Most of the time, when someone would throw javelins of words my way, they would glance off the emotional shield I raised. However, there were times when the names and words would stick into my heart like a knife. What made the difference in whether a name hurt me or not? It depended on whether I believed the name to be true. For instance, when a sibling would call me "stupid," that didn't hurt me. I knew I was as smart as most. But when they called me "pig" or "fatty," those words crushed me because I knew I was overweight. Their unkind words confirmed in me something I feared was true.

In the book of Mark, chapter 5, we read about a woman who had been stabbed repeatedly with a "name knife." It left a seething wound that only God could heal. It wasn't until she met Jesus that her life and her story were rewritten.

For 12 years this poor woman had suffered terribly with a constant hemorrhage. I have never had this problem, but I've had close friends and family members who have experienced the same plight as this woman. Causes and conditions vary with the individual, but fibrous tumors in the uterus have been known to cause this type of bleeding. Gratefully, the women I know who have suffered this malady have been blessed to have access to sound medical help. Unfortunately, this nameless woman in this biblical account had gone to her doctors, but they had not been able to alleviate or even control her condition. In fact, the Scripture tells us that she "had endured much at the hands of many physicians, and had spent all that she had and was not helped at all, but rather had grown worse" (verse 26).

Interestingly enough, as I was studying this particular passage, I came across some of the remedies this woman most likely would have been offered by her doctors. Read them and see if you think any of them would have helped her condition.

- ⊙ drinking goblets of wine containing powder compound from rubber, alum, and garden crocus
- ⊙ large doses of Persian onions
- ⊙ sudden shock therapy (I have to wonder if they used electric eels, lightning rods, or did they just scream at her while she was sleeping. Who knows?)
- ⊙ carrying the ashes of an ostrich egg in a certain cloth in her pocket[2]

Not only was this woman subjected to the loss of her health through such quackery, but she had also lost all her money in pursuit of a medical remedy. If that wasn't bad enough, this poor woman had become a victim in another way. Though her initial problems were physical and eventually financial, the result of those conditions also left her a casualty of her own religion.

Being a woman under Levitical law and having an issue of blood for all those years basically meant she had lost her ability to participate in her religious traditions. Jews were not allowed to enter the temple when they were bleeding. To complicate matters, if someone were to touch her, they too were temporarily banned from the temple. As a result, she was obligated to *rename* herself. She had to take on the burden of one of the saddest of all names noted in the Scriptures. She was to all around her, "Unclean." When someone tried to approach her space, for example, she had to tell them, "I am unclean." What an unfortunate predicament for this ailing woman. Along with everything else, she had also lost her identity. But then came the day when she heard that Jesus could change her name. He had called a simple fisherman to Himself, and changed his name to "a strong rock." He took what others had called an empty wine barrel and changed its name to "plenty." He took a "house of thieves" and changed its name back to "His Father's House." Jesus took a lame man and changed his name to "Walker." He took a demon-possessed man and changed his name to "Set Free." Certainly this healer, this restorer could do what no one else could do—rid her of the name "Unclean."

Caught in the crowd, this weak woman with the issue of blood found herself within arm's reach of Jesus. She had faith that He could help her even though all of the modern medical wisdom of her time had failed. She took the risk and touched the hem of His garment.

For the first time in years she suddenly felt strong and healthy. She knew immediately that the implications of the name she'd worn for so long was fading. Can you imagine the elation of that moment? Before she met Jesus, no one else had been able to meet her need. Everyone else had taken from her; He was the first to give to her. Before that moment when she reached out to Jesus, she was a woman desperate and destitute. All that changed in an instant.

But before she could drink in what had truly transpired, Jesus stopped, looked around, and asked, "Who touched My garments?"

Oh, no! She had been found out. By touching Jesus she made Him "unclean." The Mark passage continues, "But the woman fearing and trembling, aware of what had happened to her, came and fell down before Him and told Him the whole truth." I'm sure it must have been a relief to be able, after so much time and so much abuse, to unload her heart on someone who not only cared about her but was able to help her.

Jesus' gentle, verbal response to this hurting woman contains one of the sweetest, most healing words ever spoken. With what must have been a welcomed look of compassion, He said to her, "*Daughter,* your faith has made you well; go in peace and be healed of your affliction" (verse 34). The word "daughter" in this passage is used only this one time. The meaning of it indicates a close, loving, intimate relationship between the two of them. No longer would this woman be called "Unclean." From that moment on, her name was changed to "Daughter."

Jesus—A Friend to the Thirsty

When we observe how Jesus interacted with the women of His day, too often we are looking through our Western, twenty-first-century eyes. The very fact that Jesus took notice of these women and found them worthy of His attention was contrary to what was considered culturally acceptable behavior for His time.

For example, in John 4, Jesus spoke to a woman at a well and made a simple, even logical request of her. He said, "Let me have a drink of water." Sounds reasonable enough. However, the acceptable standard of conduct for that day would prohibit any respectable Middle Eastern man from speaking to a woman in public. Even if a man met his mother, wife, or sister on the street, he was expected to walk right past her. For all intents and purposes, women in the patriarchy of old Palestine were considered invisible.

Not only did Jesus break the rule about speaking to a woman in public, but He went well beyond what would be considered proper behavior and talked to a woman who was also a Samaritan. It was a well-known fact that the Jews hated that particular group of people. They might have had a host of reasons why they considered them hate-worthy, but the main cause of their disdain was related to the fact that Samaritans were the offspring of Jews who had chosen to intermarry with non-Jews. As a result of such unions, they were considered "half-breeds." It is said that a Jew would walk many miles out of his way to avoid letting his foot land where a Samaritan's foot might possibly have been.

One additional fact that makes Jesus talking to this person at the well so radical was she was not only a *woman,* and a *Samaritan* woman, but she was also an *immoral* woman. For most folks of that time, these reasons would have been enough to declare, "Three strikes, you're out of here." However, Jesus chose to look past her sin and reveal to her what her real problem was.

When He said to her, "Go, call your husband and come here." She replied factually, "I have no husband." Jesus said something to the effect, "You're right about that. You've had five husbands, and the one you're living with now, you didn't even bother to marry."

The response Jesus gave to this woman is much different than what my immediate reaction would call for. Jesus bypassed the obvious facts of her sin and lack of judgment in husbands. I'm afraid I would have stopped on that subject for a while and told her what I thought about how she was living her life. Most likely, I would have given her a lecture pointing out her stupidity and propensity to select "losers for lovers." When I read of the merciful compassion of Christ and contrast His response to my self-righteous reaction, I'm pressed to my knees in worship of this Savior who is so willing to love and forgive.

I find it equally curious and thoroughly refreshing that Jesus didn't focus on her sin, but went right to the heart of her need. When I read the biblical account of the Lord's exchange with this woman at the well, I can almost hear the Lord speaking to her in today's vernacular:

> You're a thirsty woman, aren't you? You come here every day looking for something to quench your thirst. But don't you realize that no water you could bring up from this well will satisfy your thirst for very long? This insufficient drinking water is not unlike the other things you're doing to try to fill up the empty places in your life.

> You've tried quenching the thirst in your soul by drinking in the attention of men who use and abuse you. I know you want to be loved, but those men are not going to gratify your longing. Aren't you tired of doing the same things over and over, only to get the same unsat- isfactory results? Let me "fill your cup" with Living Water. You don't need to live your life thirsty anymore. Let Me do for you what no human has been able to do for you.

After the life-changing exchange between Jesus and this woman, John 4:28-29 tells us that she left her waterpot and ran to tell others about the "living water" she had found. Isn't it awesome that this sinful Samaritan woman was the first evangelist to Gentiles of the Good News of Jesus, the Messiah! With this encounter with Him, she went from being a miserable sinner to a successful missionary.

Jesus—A Friend of In-Laws

I'm so glad that Jesus is the same today as He was then. He still forgives and shows mercy, even when we're guilty of the wrong of which we've been accused. He still erases the ugly names that life can tag us with, and by His grace alone, He calls us daughters. Today, Jesus still satisfies the thirsty of heart. He alone can fill the human cup of weakness with His strength and comfort.

If a mother-in-law and daughter-in-law want to take the first steps toward the destination of a healthy and enjoyable relationship, they need not go any further than following Christ. They can *do what He did* when He pardoned the adulteress and reached out to the sick woman. They can pour the same water of mercy into each other's lives that Christ poured into the soul of the woman at the well. The bridge that spans the spiritual gap has already been built. His name is Jesus. Will you cross it today and go to your mother-in-law or your daughter-in-law and let the healing begin?

My husband tells me I should be adult about the situation and just "get over it," but my feelings are so hurt. I'm not sure I'll ever feel the same toward my daughter-in-law. We went to visit our son and his wife last week. When we arrived, I discovered that our daughter-in-law was attending a mother/daughter banquet the next night at her church. Since her mother lives out of state, I thought it would be nice if the two of us attended the function together. I waited all afternoon for her to bring up the subject and invite me to go with her. Totally ignoring my presence, she began to get ready for the evening. I was crushed when she didn't ask me to go along. My husband tried to explain to our son why I was locked in the bedroom, sobbing uncontrollably. My son said he was sorry, but he refused to confront his wife with her obvious thoughtlessness. I don't know with whom I'm more upset, my daughter-in-law or my son. There's one thing I do know, I never want to go back to their house.

8

Boxers Dance, Too

It's a troubling thought that one of your most embarrassing moments could be on the occasion of meeting your future mother-in-law, but one daughter-in-law shared such a circumstance. Her accounting of this memorable day could have easily turned from comedy to conflict. She wrote,

> I had just started seriously dating my husband around the time his sister was getting married. He invited me to attend the nuptials with him. This sounded like it would be a convenient occasion to meet the rest of his family. I desperately wanted to make a good first impression on them, but I was especially concerned with what my future mother-in-law would think of me. I spent a lot of time looking for the perfect dress, fretting over what I would wear to the event.
>
> On the day of the wedding I happened to show up a little late. Consequently, I was seated close to the front of the church. When my husband's mother walked down the aisle, I was shocked to see we were wearing identical, matching dresses.
>
> It was embarrassing enough to be dressed exactly like the mother-of-the-bride, but I was even more mortified to think I had picked out the same attire as a woman forty-four years older than me.

My mother-in-law was very gracious and simply said, "My, don't we both have excellent taste!"

While the dress fiasco could have started this mother-in-law and future daughter-in-law's relationship off on the wrong foot, or should I say shoulders, it's encouraging to see that they were able to keep a sense of humor about what could have turned into an awkward situation.

Inevitably, embarrassing moments and even outright conflicts occur in in-law relationships. Sometimes the problem happens not out of a vindictive, hateful motive, but simply out of ignorance or insensitivity. For example, one daughter-in-law wrote,

> Years ago I saw the counted cross stitch sampler, *To His Mother*. It might help to understand how deeply sincere my thoughts were about her, if you knew what I stitched…
>
> My mother-in-law, they say, and yet
> Somehow I simply can't forget
> 'Twas you who watched his baby ways
> Who taught him his first hymn of praise,
> Who smiled at him my loving pride
> When he first toddled by your side
>
> My mother-in-law, but oh, 'twas you
> Who taught him to be kind and true,
> When he was tired, almost asleep
> 'Twas to your arms he used to creep
> And when he bruised his tiny knee,
> 'Twas you who kissed it tenderly.
>
> My mother-in-law, they say, and yet
> Somehow I never shall forget

How very much I owe
To you, who taught him how to grow
You trained your son to look above
You made of him, the man I love
And so I think of that today,
Ah! There with thankful heart I'll say,
...our Mother[1]

I've always had it in the back of my mind that when I had a mother-in-law I would make it for her and give it as a gift. Well, I did just as I had planned. I spent endless hours stitching the poem. I took it to a craft store and had it professionally matted and framed. It was a veritable masterpiece, if I do have to say so myself. Proudly, I presented my labor of love to my mother-in-law. I couldn't believe my eyes when I went to visit a few days later. My mother-in-law had taken the poem out of its matted frame, and she placed something her daughter had made for her in it instead. I didn't know what to think, but I knew I didn't like it one little bit.

In the following pages, mothers-in-law and daughters-in-law openly share some of their trying experiences. Among the many comments, perhaps you will find a familiar circumstance. It may be comforting to know that you are not alone in your struggle to gain peace with your in-laws.

- ☉ My mother-in-law criticized my mother's housekeeping habits.

- ☉ She offers unsolicited advice about how to clean and organize my house "a better way."

- She calls me a "good eater." I don't know how she intends for me to take that comment, but I'm insulted by it.

- She shows favoritism toward her daughter and her daughter's children.

- She pressures us to have children.

- She tells total strangers the most personal of details of our family life. I learned too late that she could not keep a confidence.

- Not only does my mother-in-law show a total disinterest in anything that's important to me, worse than that, she couldn't care less about her grandchildren. I personally look forward to being a grandmother someday, and I can't for the life of me figure out why she neglects her son's children.

- She openly compares me to her can-do-no-wrong daughter.

- She won't let me help her with the housework when we're there for a visit. However, while I'm there she's always complaining about how my sister-in-law never does anything for her or help with the dishes when she comes to see her. I have a sneaking suspicion that as soon as I leave, the same complaint is cast against me. So I've learned to not ask any more. I get up and start cleaning the dishes, even against her protest.

- She lies about things. She tends to make situations up to fit what she wants them to be. You never know if something has really happened a certain way or if someone really did what she said they did. I've learned to never get mad at anyone over something she's told me.

- She mistreated my husband terribly.

- She's jealous of the time we spend with my parents. She's so mean, I spend as little time as possible with her. However, my parents are the sweetest people in the world. I love being with them and refuse to be made to feel guilty for wanting to be with them.

⊙ She accuses me of keeping her son from coming to see her. The truth is, I have to force him to visit her by making him feel guilty. I tell him, "One of these days you're going to get a call saying she's dead. How's that going to make you feel about neglecting her?" It's infuriating to be blamed for something I don't do. If only she knew how I go to bat for her maybe she'd be nicer to me. But on the other hand, if she's not good to her own son, why do I think she'd be good to me, an "outsider."

⊙ Our child is adopted and we couldn't be happier with the precious little girl that God has given to us. My mother-in-law, on the other hand, always makes a point of talking about her friends who have "real" children and "real" grandchildren.

⊙ My in-laws never come and visit us. They expect us to make the five-hour drive every time. It's not as though their health is bad, they go every other place they want to.

⊙ She always tells people, "She took my baby from me." The sick part is, she means it. It's been 14 years; it's time to get over it.

⊙ My mother-in-law is so picky about gifts and things she gets. I try very hard to buy the perfect present for her, but she offers no response to my effort, and it's never good enough. I've spent a fortune on her, but she doesn't seem to appreciate anything I get for her.

⊙ I asked her to forgive me but she refused to accept my apology.

⊙ She punishes the grandchildren by ignoring them when she's mad at her son, their father.

⊙ She comes to visit once a year. When she came the last time she brought one of her grandchildren she sees all the time. I was very hurt and upset. Why can't she spend some special time with my children?

⊙ After both of my children started school, she called me one morning and told me it was time for me to get a job and start "pulling my own weight." I was insulted and felt like the years I had spent at home were a waste. To me being a mother was the most important thing in my life.

⊙ She always acted like she knew my husband so much better than me. She tried to make me feel jealous, and she succeeded.

⊙ My mother-in-law insisted on coming over to our house whenever she wanted to, whether it was a good time for us or not. I dreaded her visits because she was so pushy.

⊙ My husband and I ended up in counseling trying to figure out how to establish some boundaries that my mother-in-law couldn't break down.

⊙ She pretends I don't exist. She doesn't send me a birthday card or give me a Christmas present. I am absolutely invisible to her.

⊙ She would not stay out of our business. I asked my husband to confront her. He did, in his usually harsh manner. Eventually, he rejected her and asked her not to come to him as he was dying of cancer. He never made peace with her. I feel guilty for pushing my husband to "get her to back off." I fear I set in motion this whole big mess. I wish I'd kept my mouth shut.

There is one more story worthy of our reading. The following is an account of an older-but-wiser daughter-in-law who has struggled with her share of conflicting situations with an alcoholic mother-in-law. There are principles of conduct illustrated by the restraint and the positive actions of this woman named Amelia that will help in dealing with conflicts.

When my mother-in-law would come to visit us, I never knew who was going to show up. It all depended on how much she'd had to drink. Since she was an alcoholic, we soon discovered that her personality varied, thus her behavior was greatly influenced by what and how much liquor she'd consumed. In a strange way, it really helped to have something else to blame rather than to just assume she didn't love her son or his family.

My mother-in-law was a very complicated person. Although I found it terribly irritating when she introduced me to her friends as her "fat daughter-in-law," I tried to look past her steely, gruff, ill-mannered ways. It was mostly out of respect for my husband's feelings that I was willing to put up with so much mistreatment. He already felt terrible about how she acted, I didn't want to put him in an awkward position of having to confront her.

I made a concerted effort to look behind the scenes at her behavior. Even though there was no excuse for being so rude, I had to acknowledge that she had lived a very hard life. She was widowed twice, raised by a mean, hateful father, and neglected by a distracted mother. Her children had all moved away from her, and understandably so. Still she was a sad, lonely old woman who had put up a thick wall to keep out the hurt. But to her detriment, the barriers that she erected to protect herself from harm unintentionally deflected any love that happened to come her way.

It wasn't until after she died that I realized she'd never let any of us get to know the person she really was. Sadly, she died very suddenly. She walked outside to go to the mailbox one morning and dropped dead. We went into her house to tend to her affairs the same day she died. It was just as she had left it that morning. To our astonishment, we found posted notes all around the house. Over the kitchen sink was a notation reminding her to pray for her grandson. In the bathroom, tacked to the mirror was a reminder to pray for her granddaughter. On and on the notes were placed. Everyone in her family had a special spot, where she would lift them up to the Lord in prayer.

It's so strange, we thought. As many times as we had visited her, we had never seen what was going on in her heart and in her home after we left. Even though she put up a facade of distance, we now realize she really did love her family the best way she could.

Keys to Overcoming Conflict

Key 1: *Keep Your Distance*

After hearing Amelia's account, I asked her, "What did you do over the years to overcome the conflicts you experienced with your mother-in-law?" She shared what I've come to call the three keys to overcoming conflict.

"As much as I desired for my mother-in-law to be a part of our family, to know her grandchildren and enjoy her life, I came to realize that there are some people you just have to keep at arm's length. Try as you might, when that person is a destructive presence in your life you have to take measures toward self-preservation."

Amelia's first step toward making peace with her mother-in-law was an excellent example of the biblical model found in Romans 12:14-21. That passage offers some incredible wisdom for all who encounter ongoing conflicts with others. It reads:

> Bless those who persecute you; bless and do not curse. Rejoice with those who rejoice, and weep with those who weep. Be of the same mind toward one another; do not be haughty in mind, but associate with the lowly. Do not be wise in your own estimation. Never pay back evil for evil to anyone. Respect what is right in the sight of all men. *If possible, so far as it depends on you, be at peace with all men.* Never take your own revenge, beloved, but leave room for the wrath of God, for it is written, "Vengeance is mine, I will repay," says the Lord. "But if your enemy is hungry, feed him, and if he is thirsty, give him a drink; for in so doing you will heap burning coals on his head." Do not be overcome by evil, but overcome evil with good (emphasis added).

This admonition from God's Word offers some incredibly important wisdom for anyone who encounters ongoing conflict with others. I particularly appreciate verse 18, which reminds us that we are limited in our ability to produce peace in some instances: "If possible, so far as it depends on you, be at peace with all men." God acknowledges that there are some people who will refuse to be pleasant and peaceable. This verse is not an excuse to stop trying to show love toward a disagreeable in-law. An individual can do all the praying in the world, but if the other person refuses to listen to God, then the fact must be faced that there is a limit to what can be done to reach her heart.

Even with this passage in mind, Amelia continued to keep in touch with her mother-in-law. She said,

> Our family sent cards on her birthday, gifts for the holidays, called her on a regular basis, and visited her as much as we thought wise. When we went to see her, we tried to keep her limitations in mind. Since she was used to being alone, we knew that bringing small children into her home made her very nervous. She worried about her little knickknacks getting broken, so we decided it was best if we met in a more "child friendly" environment. The McDonald's playground became a comfortable spot for a short, noisy visit. The children could eat, play, and make messes, and it didn't harm our relationship. Sometimes we would choose to meet at a local park. There she was free to watch the children play without concern for her flower garden, her pets, or her possessions.

This daughter-in-law must be commended for her unselfish efforts at bridging the in-law gap. Much to her credit, she had learned that "keeping her distance" physically didn't necessitate cutting the mother-in-law off from their love.

Key 2: *Keep Your Tongue*

Thankfully, Amelia's story contains a second step to over-coming conflict. Along with keeping a safe distance and taking precautions to make what time that is spent together pleasant, it is also imperative that we keep a watch over our words. Amelia continued,

> After my mother-in-law died, I was especially glad I had bitten my tongue on more than one occasion. Believe me, I can't count how many times I wanted to blast right back at her when she said things to me that hurt my feelings. Of course, I didn't like her critical spirit when it was aimed my way, but nothing upset me more than when she would berate my husband. In all fairness, she was meaner to him than she ever was to me.
>
> Keeping my tongue in control was, and is, one of the most serious lessons in humility I have dealt with. There were times when everything in me would want to scream, "You can't talk to me like that." However, I discovered that when I was willing to hold back revengeful, cutting words, God then would supply the strength to control them.

Amelia was a living example of one who wisely accepted the truth found in Proverbs 18:21: "Death and life are in the power of the tongue, and those who love it will eat its fruit." When we're willing to humble ourselves before the Lord and submit to the authority of His Word by obeying it, then we are in the best position possible. Isaiah 66:2 says, "But to this one I will look, to him who is *humble* and *contrite of spirit*, and who *trembles at My word*" (emphasis added).

Key 3: Keep Smiling

When it comes to family relationships, what Amelia finally chose to do reminds us that we have access to a divine alternative that has the potential to heal weary hearts. Ultimately, she realized she could either learn to *laugh* at her unpleasant situation or she could *lambaste* the one who was stepping on her toes during her tedious in-law dance.

Though not always easy to find, Amelia managed to root out some lighter moments in her relationship with her mother-in-law. By doing so, the heaviness of tension was relieved… somewhat.

> My efforts to bring some levity into the situation was sort of one-sided, actually. Not much humor came my way. Instead, I was regular in delivering "the goods." I began to cut out funny stories out of magazines, cartoons out of newspapers, and copied humorous e-mails that others would send me. When I'd go visit, I'd take an envelope stuffed with funnies and give them to her. Sometimes she'd read them while I was there and, to my amazement, I would hear her quietly chuckle at a few of the things. It was somehow medicinal to hear her when she'd tentatively giggle. To be honest, the humor I found from it all was just knowing that I really did "get to her."

We have the same choice that Amelia had. The book of Proverbs gives us some good reasons to keep a sense of humor. Chapter 15, verse 13 reminds us that "a joyful heart makes a cheerful face." Forget about the laugh lines and go for it! Also we are told in verse 15, "A cheerful heart has a continual feast." Oops! There goes the waistline…but it's O.K. to keep laughing because "a joyful heart is good medicine, but a broken spirit dries up the bones" (Proverbs 17:22).

Sometimes it takes time for us to see the humor in a situation. Here's a "now it's funny" story shared by a daughter-in-law. She's talking about her first visit to her in-laws.

My husband and I were married in my hometown in the heart of the Midwest. After the wedding, we drove east to spend a few days with my husband's family. I had only met his parents twice before, and they hadn't taken the 1500-mile trip for the wedding. So we were going to have a reception at their home for my husband's friends and family.

We spent the first night of our visit with my new in-laws in my husband's childhood bedroom. The next morning we dressed and sheepishly went into the kitchen for breakfast. My mother-in-law was busily serving up the food, and my father-in-law was sipping coffee at the kitchen table. It was a hot and humid day, and so all four of us were in our bare feet. We sat down and began to eat.

Under the table next to my foot, I could feel the brush of my new husband's hairy foot. So, I inched my toes up the side of his foot, and began playing "footsie," sometimes even stroking his ankle with my foot. Funny thing, he never looked up at me. *He must be shy*, I thought.

Soon the meal was done, and my mother-in-law got up to clear the table. My husband then excused himself and got up to help her, and I was still stroking his foot!

To my horror I realized it was my father-in-law's foot! I shot a glance at him, and jerked my foot away. He continued to stare, stone-faced at his plate, not saying a word, as he had done the entire meal. I wanted the earth to open up and swallow me.

It took three years before I could bring myself to tell my husband what I had done. And my in-laws have never brought up the subject, either.

For nearly 20 years I was a faithful wife and loving mother. I never even considered being unfaithful to my husband. Together we had a wonderful marriage with four beautiful children. We served the Lord as a family. Two years ago my husband met a woman at work. She was a seductress and he, to my astonishment, was a fool.

As a result of his choices, he has abandoned our family and has moved in with her. All of this would be tragic enough, but to add to the unbearable pain, my in-laws have turned against me and forsaken my children. Never in a million years would I have ever dreamed they would treat us that way.

Even though my father-in-law and my mother-in-law are dedicated, wonderful Christians, they have decided to uphold their son in his sinful lifestyle and turn against me. He is living with this woman and has a baby out of wedlock. Yet you would think I'm the one who has destroyed their grandchildren's lives and disgraced the family name. It looks as though they consider anything he does as fine. I'm so terribly disappointed in them. They have embraced this hussy and shunned me. It's not fair. Sometimes I just want to move away, take my children with me, and never lay eyes on my in-laws again. Was the love they showed me for all those years nothing but a joke?

9

Trading Partners

The dance between a mother-in-law and daughter-in-law can be challenging under the best of circumstances. As I stated earlier, the relationship between these two women can be the most fragile of all human connections. Sadly enough, when the destructiveness of a divorce is added to the mix, the love bond between the mother-in-law and the daughter-in-law will falter, turning this unique dance into a very wobbly waltz.

Nothing is easy or natural when it comes to dealing with the aftermath of divorce. When Jesus was asked about permitting a certificate of divorcement allowing for the negating of a marriage, He indicated that this was not a part of the original plan of God. In Matthew 19:3-8, Jesus quotes from the Old Testament reminding us of God's initial intentions.

> Some Pharisees came to Jesus, testing Him and asking, "Is it lawful for a man to divorce his wife for any reason at all?" And He answered and said, "Have you not read that He who created them from the beginning made them male and female, and said 'for this reason a man shall leave his father and mother and be joined to his wife, and the two shall become one flesh'? So, they are no longer two, but one flesh. What therefore God has joined together, let no man separate." They said to Him, "Why then did

Moses command to give her a certificate of divorce and send her away?" He said to them, "Because of your hardness of heart Moses permitted you to divorce your wives; but from the beginning it has not been this way."

As Jesus stated to the Pharisees, divorce was not in the original plan for marriage. God only allowed it because of unrepentant, hardened hearts. Therefore, the dissolving of a marriage union is outside God's perfect plan. And for all intents and purposes, divorce is not even supposed to exist. Consequently, any solution to the dilemmas that are bound to arise as a result of this tragedy will be incomplete and inadequate.

It is undeniable that the mother-in-law truly faces a no-win predicament when her son and his wife separate. Every divorce situation is complicated and hurtful, but none more so for the mother-in-law than when it is her son who has wrongly left his marriage and wounded his wife and children. Too often she is left with the impossible situation of either having to accept the unacceptable or face the possibility of losing contact with her son. She may even at times find herself violating her own sense of morality by giving *approval* to the heartbreaking choices her son is making. In order to keep the connection with him, she will often turn her back on the former daughter-in-law whom she may have sincerely loved. Given these complications, is it any wonder why God says, "I hate divorce" (Malachi 2:16).

A recently divorced daughter-in-law sadly said,

> My mother-in-law and I were really good friends. She was such a great help to me when I gave birth to the children. Through the years, we've

spent a lot of time laughing, praying, and planning family events together. It really hurts me
to see how she's turned her back on me and the
grandchildren. I know she loves her son, and
she can't be blamed for the bad choices he's
made, but I can't help but think that if she hadn't
given him her approval of his lifestyle choices,
he may have thought twice about throwing his
family away. As close as we were, I haven't spoken to her in two years. She lives just down the
road from me, and she hasn't called my children
in months. Who would have ever thought it
would have turned out this way?

Not all mother-in-law and daughter-in-law relationships fall
apart when the marriage does. A heartbroken, yet determined,
mother-in-law spoke to me after a mother/daughter tea where
I was the guest speaker. Hoping to cheer her daughter-in-law
up, she had brought her to the event. She said, "I have the
most incredible daughter-in-law in the whole world. She and
my son are going through a terrible divorce. He is an alcoholic
and is prone to treat her cruelly. I've encouraged her to get
out of the situation before she gets hurt any more than she
already has. She knows that I'm there for her and always will
be."

To be honest, I was amazed at the strength and determi-
nation this mother-in-law demonstrated. Recognizing the strong
bond that I feel with my own son, I can only hope that if I
were in her position I would have as clear a sense of what to
do to help my daughter-in-law. I asked her the question that
was pressing on my mind. "Is it difficult to align yourself with

your daughter-in-law and thus set yourself opposite your own son?"

The lady responded with obvious concern for her son but with equal conviction of the correctness of her actions. "Absolutely not! Right is right, and wrong is wrong. What my son is doing is destructive to himself and to his entire family. If I give him my approval, then I'm actually encouraging him to live in such a way that will destroy him. I love him too much to let him think what he's doing is all right. My daughter-in-law has been a faithful wife and loving mother. She's done nothing to warrant the kind of treatment she has received at his hand." To say the least, I was amazed by this brave woman's answer.

Some very respectable women who have felt the sting that comes from the slap of divorce were kind enough to share words from their hearts about their pain. I hope their candid words will encourage those of you who may be experiencing loss because of divorce.

⊙ My grandson needs me more now than he ever has. His parents are going through a divorce, and his little world has come unraveled. I let my daughter-in-law know that she can depend on me to help in any way she wants me to. I don't want to get in the middle of the problems she and my son are having. I do, however, want to be a good grandmother to my grandson. I appreciate all that she's allowed me to do for both of them.

⊙ My granddaughter was disappointed when I didn't send her mother a birthday card this year. When my son and his wife divorced, I broke off all contact with my daughter-in-law. We didn't really get along that well when she and my son were married, and I was not under the delusion that things would improve now that they are divorced. However, I was really moved when I saw the sadness on my granddaughter's face.

⊙ My mother-in-law has pulled away from my children. I don't think she can see a way to have a relationship with them because they are so closely connected to me. It's terribly sad. Everyone loses this way.

⊙ My mother-in-law has remained impartial to the marital problems between me and her son. She welcomed me into the family from day one and has loved me as a daughter. She was always my friend and still is 22 years later.

⊙ I never said disrespectful things about my husband in the presence of his mother or to anyone else in his family. I knew my mother-in-law didn't want to hear her son talked down any more than I would want someone talking badly about my boy.

⊙ My mother-in-law really loved her first daughter-in-law. When my husband and I were first married, I was constantly told by my mother-in-law what good taste my husband's former wife had in clothes and home decorating. I learned very quickly how well she could cook, keep house, and how much fun the two of them had together. After a while I realized that when my mother-in-law started talking about the other woman, I needed to change the subject or just get up and leave the room. I can't emotionally take being compared to her anymore. If she was such an incredible person, why didn't my husband stay married to her? I don't think I can ever be close to my mother-in-law.

⊙ A daughter-in-law pleaded for her mother-in-law to stay out of the marriage and keep her opinions to herself. She added, "If worse comes to worse and the marriage ends in divorce, then stay out of it. In the long run, this approach will work out better for everyone."

⊚ A mother-in-law pleaded for her daughter-in-law to leave her out of the situation and stop making her choose sides. She said, "Unless you are being physically hurt, don't use me as a 'go-between' for you and my son. As much as I care about you, please keep me out of it, and don't tell me what's going on. I'm not the one you should be confiding in at this point. When you cry and tell me things that my son's doing to you and the children, it puts me in an impossible position. I'm afraid you will eventually regret the things you say to me in hurt or in haste. I love you, but I don't need to know the details."

As I asked mothers-in-law and daughters-in-law about what happens to their relationship when a divorce occurs between the son and the wife, some reccurring themes surfaced. There are at least three things these ladies encourage others to keep in mind if or when they find themselves in this horrible situation. Hopefully, you will never need this chapter of the book, but if you or someone you love does, perhaps the following suggestions will be helpful.

Guard Against Assigning Blame

Even though it had been quite a few years since the divorce was finalized, Tina's face revealed the depth of hurt buried right under the surface as she told her story.

> Of course the disgrace and humiliation of my husband's public betrayal of me was bad enough, but what I wasn't prepared for was the attitude of my in-laws.

From the time I met them, they openly embraced and accepted me as Jim's wife. For all these years we have gone to church together, had Sunday lunch each week, and have shared the best of times during holiday celebrations and family vacations.

When Jim had the affair with the other woman, no one who knew him could believe he had done it. And furthermore, no one was more shocked than me. When the facts of his illicit relationship became known, I went to my in-laws expecting them to comfort and shield the children and me from the unbelievable harm that their son had inflicted on us. To my surprise and horror, they sided with Jim. Even more heartbreaking, all of a sudden I was portrayed as a bad wife.

I felt the smack of blame as they accused me for all the trouble. They said the reason Jim had left me for the other woman was because I wasn't a good housekeeper and I didn't have sex with him as often as I should have. None of these accusations were true. But what if they had been? When did leaving a ring around the bathtub or dishes in the sink become justifiable grounds for adultery and divorce? Jim must have told them bold, bare-faced lies, and they chose to believe him. I felt as though my in-laws questioned my character and morality instead of my husband's.

When I heard the hurt in Tina's voice, I was reminded once again just how far-reaching the effect of sin goes and how many people it destroys. One of the age-old responses to sin is blaming someone else. Jim's parents were desperate to believe that their son was not really as bad as he seemed and that he was not responsible for his actions. Perhaps by shifting the blame from Jim onto Tina they could come to some sort of peace with what he was doing. Regardless of their intentions, the result was additional, unnecessary hurt to Tina.

Oh, the unspeakable damage we do to one another when, instead of extending a merciful pardon, we activate the guillotine of judgment. To illustrate how choosing to show mercy over judgment can heal a relationship, consider the story of one mother-in-law whose son and his wife were going through a terrible divorce. When she was put to the excruciating challenge of choosing judgment over mercy, she found a way to guard against judging her daughter-in-law. She opted to deal with the hurtful aftermath of separation and divorce.

> As I prayed about the tragic situation, the Lord reminded me of the truths found in 2 Corinthians 10:3-5. I made it my determination to live according to this admonition. The passage says, "For though we walk in the flesh, we do not war according to the flesh, for the weapons of our warfare are not of the flesh, but divinely powerful for the destruction of fortresses. We are destroying speculations and every lofty thing raised up against the knowledge of God, and we are taking every thought captive to the obedience of Christ."
>
> When I'm tempted to speculate on why my son or my daughter-in-law has said or done something that hurts me and those I love, I simply choose to take my thoughts captive to the obedience of Christ. I have learned that when I choose to give over to the temptation of judging them and when I make assumptions about what's going on in this marriage, I find myself

paralyzed with grief and unable to trust the Lord the way I should.

Recognizing that this battle for my son and his family is a "spiritual one," I need to fight with the proper equipment. The most effective weapon is prayer. Assigning motive and standing in judgment of others only neutralizes the real influence I can have. I am to pray and allow God to work in those places where my words, anger, and imagination cannot reach. I have come to understand that my most effective stance for this battle is on my knees. Furthermore, James 2:13 says, "For judgment will be merciless to one who has shown no mercy; mercy triumphs over judgment." Since I am pleading for mercy in this potential disaster, I am expected, according to God's Word, to offer it to others. What better person to show mercy to than my precious daughter-in-law.

Guard Against Accusing Words

What is the evidence of a nonjudgmental attitude? The words we use and don't use will tell us where our heart is. We are reminded in Matthew 15:18 that the mouth is the divine tattletale of the heart. The verse reads, "But the things that proceed out of the mouth come from the heart, and those defile the man."

Keeping a heart tender toward the Lord and those around us will help us keep our words seasoned with grace, kindness, and understanding. When a mother-in-law and daughter-in-law are willing to see life from the other's viewpoint, it will help them keep a clear conscience and a sweet tongue. One thing that will help them see life from the other's perspective is to recognize what they have in common. In the case of Tina's story, the one thing that she and her mother-in-law had most in common was the incredible loss they both had experienced.

Loss: A Long, Lonely Road for a Spouse

Here are a few of the losses Tina suffered by the selfish decisions of her husband.

1. She lost the man who had promised to always be her husband, friend, confidant, and lover. Because of his decisions, Tina was left alone, lonely, and wounded.

2. She lost the man who had promised to be an ever-present father to her children. He had promised when they decided to have children that he would help shoulder the daily responsibilities of parenting. But instead of being there to guide and direct their lives every day, he would now be there every other weekend or when it was convenient to his new lifestyle.

3. She lost her partner who had promised to join their efforts in creating financial security for the family. Instead of enjoying the fruit of their joint labor, she now faced fiscal hardships.

4. She lost the man who had promised to share their future together. He was the one with whom she was going to grow old. Holidays, vacations, their children's weddings, graduations, special occasions were all changed. Christmas used to be fun and something the family enjoyed celebrating. Now, it's "just another day to try to get through."

5. She lost her trust. The man who had promised so much, changed his mind. She is left to wonder if their entire marriage was just a mirage, a pretense, a lie.

In their book *Women Under Stress*, Randy and Nanci Alcorn list the biggest stresses in a person's life. Number two, right under the death of a spouse, is divorce. Divorce takes a terrible toll on a family. In some instances, years of stability are shattered by this one decision to dissolve the marriage.

Loss: A Two-Lane Road for In-Laws

The daughter-in-law and her family suffer horrible loss. However, it's important for the daughter-in-law to recognize that the mother-in-law has suffered incredible devastation as well. Here are a few of the things Tina's mother-in-law loses as a result of the decisions made by her son.

1. She loses the dream of whom she thought her son was. Though it was not an easy conclusion for her to come to, Tina admitted, "Jim's parents thought he was the 'golden-haired prince' who could do no wrong. Oddly enough, I felt the same way. I thought he was as wonderful as his parents did. Sadly, we were both wrong. The shattered belief that their son was totally incapable of being so foolish as to throw away his wife and children, his reputation, and good standing in the church and community must have been difficult for them to accept."

2. She loses the assurance that her grandchildren are safe and protected. Their welfare was jeopardized by the actions of her son. She's left with the sad reality that her grandchildren have joined the ranks of so many other children who are victims of a broken home. Access to the grandchildren is either restricted or even prohibited as a result of the complications of divorce. Oh, what incalculable loss.

3. She loses the vision of her future. Never again, for example, will holiday celebrations and family occasions be without

complications. To muddy the waters even more, if there's a remarriage the blending of families and hearts can prove difficult.

4. She, too, loses trust. There is no way to come out of a divorce situation without feelings of hurt and disappointment.

Can a mother-in-law and a daughter-in-law overcome the trauma of divorce and maintain a loving relationship between the two of them? Some of the ladies with whom I spoke or who sent me questionnaires believed it was extremely difficult to continue a meaningful relationship beyond the divorce. There were others, however, who were more optimistic about the prospect of maintaining a love bond. One daughter-in-law offered a ray of hope in the midst of the cloud of divorce. She quipped, "My mother-in-law and I had an agreement. In the case of divorce, I got her in the settlement!" Those I spoke with who had firmly held to their belief that their friendship could survive divorce agreed that it was only possible when each of the women were willing to live according to the life-changing wisdom of Philippians 2:2-5,7. The apostle Paul writes,

> Make my joy complete by being of the same mind, maintaining the same love, united in spirit, intent on one purpose. Do nothing from selfishness or empty conceit, but with humility of mind regard one another as more important than yourselves; do not merely look out for your own personal interests, but also for the interests of others. Have this attitude in yourselves which was also in Christ Jesus... [who] emptied Himself, taking the form of a bond-servant.

Can this really happen? Can a mother-in-law and daughter-in-law really treat each other the way this passage describes when there are so many hurt feelings, broken hearts, and failed expectations? I believe so! But just like any dance, the mother-in-law and daughter-in-law reel has to have a leader.

In chapter two of this book, I proposed that the one who takes the lead in the in-law dance should, without question, be the mother-in-law. She is to *lead by backing off* and allowing her son and his wife room enough to maneuver and establish their own family. This principle is never more applicable than in the situation where the son and his wife are having marital difficulties. However, there are those critical times when the mother-in-law's part in "the dance" is to step forward and offer a hand of help and compassion to a daughter-in-law who may be sinking into the sea of despair.

It is at those times when the mother-in-law is to become a bridge-builder in the relationship. Just as the integrity of a physical bridge structure is vitally important to the safety of the span, when it comes to family relationships the strength and maturity needed to bridge the gap between a mother-in-law and a daughter-in-law can be great. I appeal to mothers-in-law to step up to the job as quiet, loving bridges to their daughters-in-law who are reaching out for a hand of support.

And what does a mother-in-law do if it is the daughter-in-law who has wielded the death blow to her marriage and crushed the heart of the mother-in-law's son and his children? The natural instinct when someone hurts our children or grandchildren is to take on the personification of a she-bear and start devouring anything and anyone in our path. The thought of someone wounding our children is painful beyond description. It is at those times of greatest distress that we must be diligent to keep God's Word in our hearts and on our minds. Referring back to the passage in 2 Corinthians 10:3, we must remember that our war is not against flesh and blood (our in-law) but against the enemy of our families that desires to destroy us all—especially the innocent little children who are caught in the middle.

Without question, it is imperative that the mother-in-law continue to focus on the fact that Satan is seeking to gobble up her family. She must stand in prayer for her son and his children and fortify herself against the fruit of evil. This is the most powerful thing she can do in the face of this horrible situation.

The sin of adultery and abandonment of the family is not a gender issue. Contrary to what we might hear or see in our pop culture of made-for-TV movies, where it seems that all women are portrayed are virtuous victims and all men are perverted pigs, it is not just men who are capable of playing the fool and leaving their families devastated. Women are just as apt to make bad choices. Assigning blame is not the answer and neither is using accusing words. The weapon of prayer will do more to defeat the enemy of our families than taking sides and throwing barbs of hurtful comments. These things only contribute to the hurt of the children.

Guard Against Acting Unkindly

The telltale sign that the mother-in-law and daughter-in-law relationship is Christ-honoring, even in the face of the stressfulness of divorce, will be revealed by the acts of kindness offered and accepted between the two women. For instance, the mother-in-law should call and check on the daughter-in-law to make sure she's all right. An offer to bring food over to the house, to help out financially with the needs of the grandchildren, and to watch the kids so she can have a break from the responsibility will do much to bridge the deepest of chasms. It is not enough for a mother-in-law to simply verbalize her regrets over what her son did or did not do, but putting feet and hands to her words will prove extremely healing to the strained relationship. Keeping her connection with her son separate from that of the daughter-in-law is essential if the mother-in-law is going to keep contact with them both.

Is she taking sides against the son by maintaining contact and being sweet and understanding with the daughter-in-law? Absolutely not. Instead of choosing against her son, she is helping extend Christ's love to his family.

The mother-in-law has two choices. She can either build a bridge or she can construct a wall. We are always constructing one or the other. One mother-in-law who chose to build a wall said, "The moment our son and his wife divorced, we were through with her. Since there were no children we had no reason to ever speak to her again. It's been five years, and I don't even know where she is."

That's one way of handling the divorce situation. However, very often there are children involved. Tragically, the same attitude is used even though it means losing contact with the grandchildren. Most of us would find that alternative completely unacceptable.

If a mother-in-law wants to have a relationship with her grandchildren, she needs to recognize the need to get out the dancing shoes, dust them off, and start learning a few new steps around the construction site. There's a bridge that needs to be built, and with God's help and using Philippians 2 as the blueprint, it can be erected.

10

Dance Lessons

I hope you have discovered a renewed sense of hope and comfort in your in-law relationships. Often, just being reminded that we are not alone in our struggle to make sense of the intricate nature of the in-law relationships can be all we need. As I conclude this book I want to offer you some additional stories and helpful suggestions that mothers-in-law and daughters-in-law have generously shared with me. It is my sincere hope that you will find one or more of these following ideas applicable to your life and thus assist you as you grow closer and closer to your in-law.

For example, I received one very special letter from a daughter-in-law who loved her in-law with the "Ruth and Naomi" kind of love moved me to tears. This letter gave me a sense of hope that the mother-in-law/daughter-in-law dance can be executed with love and grace when both women make the unselfish effort to treat one another with love.

> My mother-in-law was absolutely the best. She was one of those rare individuals who actually accepted others for who and what they were without offering criticism or judgment. When my husband brought me to meet his parents for the first time, we had known each other for 16 years, but only as close friends. I had come to Tennessee to live closer to him because I was recently divorced and had two small children.

149

I had to travel for my job and my friend James (now my husband), was the only person I could trust to be with the children while I had to be out of town. However, once I got here, our friendship began to grow into something more serious. I knew that James had told his family that we were dating, and I was very nervous about meeting them—especially his mother. I thought she would not be very receptive to a divorced woman with two small children complicating her son's life by dating him. I couldn't have been more wrong.

She welcomed me with open arms. That first night that we had dinner at her home she told me that after watching me with the children, she was impressed with what a good mother I was. She told me the children could call her Grandma Grace. She went on to tell me that James had spoken of me often over the years, and now she understood why he regarded me as such a fine person. I almost cried. I felt her warm embrace like a blanket straight out of the dryer wrapped around me in her loving words and attitude.

Grace made it a point to arrange the opportunity for me to sing at her church whenever we went to see them. This was important to me, as I had once sung professionally but had gotten away from it. She supported and encouraged me in my musical interest. She was my biggest fan.

When I had been in Tennessee about three months, she called James and told him that he needed to go on and propose to me because she thought that my children and I were the best thing that ever happened to him. I literally could do no wrong in Grace's eyes.

Even when we didn't agree on something, she never imposed her will or opinion on me. I naturally responded to her kindness with a great deal of love and respect for her.

James and I were married in her church. She had been in a wheelchair the whole time I had known her, but she had secretly practiced getting up. She walked with her husband and my husband's brother at our wedding. It was the first and last time I ever saw her stand. It meant so much to me that she would try so hard to make that day special for James and me.

When my mother-in-law became gravely ill, I stayed at the hospital with her around the clock, out of love for what she had given me in the way of support and unconditional acceptance. I read to her from a book on angels and talked to her about how much I loved her and her son. I wanted her to know how much I appreciated her. Three days before she died, she slipped into a coma.

I was there when she died and I was grateful to have had that personal time with her. I wanted to give her the support she had given me for all those years.

The following pages are more stories women have generously shared with me. I'm sure they will inspire you even as they motivated me to try to make my mother-in-law/daughter-in-law dance more graceful. In addition, I have included a few humorous stories that I hope will brighten and lighten your day.

Great Dance Step Ideas

⊙ On my husband's birthday, I sent my mother-in-law a dozen red roses. Along with the flowers I included a card expressing my sincere appreciation for all she had done for him. I told her it was because of her diligence in raising her son that I was blessed with the best man in the whole world.

I had sensed a wall between my mother-in-law and me since the early days of my marriage to her son. For some reason she acted rather cold, distant, and sometimes even competitive toward me. However, after she received the flowers and the card, she dramatically changed. Never again did she withhold her affection from me. Our relationship began to evolve into what I had always hoped it would be.

Looking back, I suppose she just wanted to be acknowledged and appreciated for the sacrifices she had made in giving me her son. She was right, she had indeed gifted me with the most wonderful of men.

⊙ Whenever my husband and I go to visit his parents, I always take a small gift (homemade cookies, nut bread, a candle, note cards) to my mother-in-law. That tiny, inexpensive gesture seems to brighten her day and has contributed to the closeness of our relationship. It's amazing what a bit of thoughtfulness can do to enhance a relationship. Also, I'm terrible about remembering to send thank-you cards after a visit. I've found that when I take the card with me, write it out, and place it on my pillow, I can leave with a clear mind and lighter heart. I've found the insignificant acts of kindness can make a tremendous difference in the mother-in-law and daughter-in-law love connection.

⊙ Each fall I invite my daughter and my daughter-in-law out for a "shoe day." With a $50 limit, my treat, they can purchase a pair of shoes, a sweater, or whatever they might happen to want or need. Of course, if they can't find exactly what they want, they can "stash the cash" until they find what suits them. This has become a tradition we all look forward to.

⊙ I invited my daughter-in-law and three of her friends to come to my house for a lovely tea party. I made a special effort to keep as quiet as possible so I could listen and learn what's on these young women's minds. As I've gotten older, it seems the generation gap has had a tendency to widen. The tea party was one of the ways I've tried to bridge the age-divide between me and my daughter-in-law's generation. I really do enjoy hearing the "young ones" talk and laugh. I want to do it again, and I hope my daughter-in-law and her friends want to come back.

⊙ My in-laws call us every Sunday evening. We have a preset time that works for all of us. Since we look forward to our conversation time, catching up with all that's happening in the extended family, we plan for our "phone time" each week. If there's a movie or television program that we want to watch, and it happens to coincide with our scheduled call, we have a videotape ready to record the show. That way, we can concentrate on our visit and relax as we talk to my husband's parents. This bit of planning and preparation eases the tension when the phone rings. When my in-laws call, I never want to be guilty of thinking, "Oh, no, not them, not now!"

⊙ I suggested to my mother-in-law that we make a past-and-present quilt. Using cloth from my husband's childhood clothes and cloth from my son's out-grown attire, we hope to create an heirloom that we can treasure for years to come.

⊙ My mother-in-law is a native of Russia. Since she's an older lady, she was intimidated at the thought of learning to speak English at her advanced age. So, I've decided to learn to speak her language. Every time I attempt to say a new word or phrase, it seems to really please her. She's also very patient with my lack of skill in pronouncing some of the more difficult sounds.

⊙ My husband is a real sweety, but he's not always as thoughtful as he should be. Therefore, I've taken on the responsibility to make sure he acknowledges my mother-in-law's birthday, Christmas, and Mother's Day. I go to the store, buy the card and gift, bring it to him, stick it in his face, and insist on him signing it. Then I mail it out to his mom. My mother-in-law is very impressed with her son's newfound thoughtfulness. I'm glad it makes her happy. I'll never be the one to tell her that it's really me who's doing it.

⊙ From the first time I met my mother-in-law, she had severe medical problems. As she got older, her condition worsened. About two months before she died, the doctor sent her home from the hospital with no hope of recovery. Since I was an experienced registered nurse, the family looked to me for advice and assistance. Even though my family could ill afford it, I took a leave of absence from my job, moved several states away, and took care of her until her passing. During the weeks prior to her death, we grew very close to one another. She was so ill she didn't say much, but I could tell she appreciated what I was doing for her. I know my husband and his siblings were relieved knowing that everything possible was done to keep their mother comfortable.

⊙ The day I came home from having our first child, my mother-in-law came to my house to take care of the baby and me. Since my mother lived out of state, I had no one else to help me. My mother-in-law couldn't have treated me any better than if she were my mom. I'll always remember how kind she was to me.

⊙ I love it when my daughter-in-law invites my husband and me over for dinner. When I see the table set so beautifully with her best dishes and linens, it makes me feel really special and very loved. But of all the nice things she does for me, the best thing is that she treats my son so lovingly. I can tell he's happy and, of course, that thrills me.

⊙ My mother-in-law and I went away for a weekend. When the trip was suggested (it was her idea!), I had my doubts about the wisdom of the plan. I didn't think we had anything in common, and I worried about what we would do or talk about. But not long into the trip I discovered we actually shared a lot of similar interests. Each time we stopped at an antique store, it seemed we gravitated toward the same items to admire. At the end of the weekend, we couldn't wait to schedule another trip. Just think, if we hadn't taken the chance, we might never have realized just how much we had in common. It was neat to realize that I would probably be this woman's friend even if she weren't my mother-in-law. Being related to her simply makes our friendship doubly enjoyable!

⊙ I tried and tried to buy Christmas gifts that my mother-in-law would like. But each selection I carefully shopped for was either the wrong size, a bad color, or just not to her taste. I couldn't seem to tune into her wavelength for gifts. Each year, by the time the holidays were over, I would feel all rung out and used up. So, I decided to do something different. I chose to send my mother-in-law a gift basket, and it's turned out to be a great success. For the past few years I've tried to select a different theme. One year, for instance, I sent her a basket with items she could use when she took her nightly bubble bath. In the basket I included some body lotions, bath oils, candles, and a lovely, soothing tape of music. Maybe she has learned to pretend to like my gifts, or I've tapped into the fact that she likes a lot of small gifts rather than one big one. Either way, I'm happier and she seems more content. I'm glad I didn't give up all together.

⊙ My mother-in-law and I had just left the grocery store and were heading home. It was warm outside and so we had the windows down. On our way, a bee flew in through the window of our car. We both started screaming as we frantically began swatting at the winged intruder. My mother-in-law, who was driving, was in a panic trying to kill the bee. A couple of times she even ran off the road. I was holding a pie in my hands, in order to keep it safe. When I took a swing at the bee, I accidentally smashed the pie into my mother-in-law's face. Unbeknownst to us, my mother-in-law's insurance agent was driving the car directly behind us. Seeing the erratic swerving of the car and the swinging of the arms inside the vehicle, he followed us home to make sure we were all right. The embarrassing truth is, he could see the battle that was going on inside the car, but he couldn't see the bee.

⊙ My parents met my soon-to-be in-laws at a restaurant. I was a little nervous because my mother is legendary for spilling her food during her meals. However, my mom did fine. It was my mother-in-law who had the problem. She not only dropped her food down her blouse, but she also choked and began coughing. She sent the contents of her mouth sailing across the table right into my mother's face. Of course, this happened after my mother-in-law squirted my mom with a lemon. It was a great way to break in our relationship.

⊙ Before I married my husband, he took me to meet his mom and sisters. They lived in a trailer park in Florida. It didn't take me long to realize that my in-laws were bona fide "night owls." I am a morning person, so staying up late into the wee hours of the night is not my cup of tea. In fact, when I become sleep deprived, I'm not exactly the nicest person to be around. I went to bed earlier in the evening, but my husband and his mom and sisters' constant laughing and loud talking kept me awake. Totally frustrated and irritable from lack of sleep, I burst from the bedroom and stormed out of the trailer and into the night. Since I left without explaining that I was going for a short walk, just to clear my mind, a few minutes later they all came out searching for me. Horrified at the embarrassing situation I had set in motion, I hid in the bushes. For some weird reason, I thought if I stayed out of sight long enough, they would go back into the trailer, and I could simply meander back in, as though nothing had happened. That plan was short-lived when I realized they were not going to give up on their quest to find me. In fact, they were enlisting others to come help in the search. It was one of my most embarrassing moments when I had to show myself and try to explain why I'd acted the way I did. My husband and I have been married for five years. I'm amazed that he still wanted to marry me after the way I acted.

My prayer is that God will help you in "the dance" of loving your in-laws. As we learn to get along with our extended families, we should be blessed to know that in-laws are another way God provides more folks with whom we can give and receive love.

Dance Rehearsals
A Study Guide

1
May I Have This Dance

When it comes to our in-laws, we have little or no say in who becomes a part of our family. Therefore, it behooves us to quickly learn to embrace those whom God has brought into our lives by love and by law. In order to gracefully "dance" with your in-law, reread the account found in Ruth 1:16-17. Perhaps the New Living Translation will lend an even more simplified beauty to this ancient declaration of love between a mother-in-law and her daughter-in-law:

> Don't ask me to leave you or turn back. I will go wherever you go and live wherever you live. Your people will be my people, and your God will be my God. I will die where you die and will be buried there. May the LORD punish me severely if I allow anything but death to separate us!

What struggles do you face in learning to love and accept your in-law? List three things you must put aside in order to learn to love more fully.

1.

2.

3.

Pray and ask the Lord to show you how to put on a heart of compassion. What three things could you do to get your feelings more in line with the way God would have you treat your in-law?

1.

2.

3.

What is the biggest hindrance between how you *feel* and how you want to *act* toward your in-law?

2
Who Is Supposed to Lead?

Without a doubt, being a mother entails much more than just being a "rented womb" for approximately nine months. No, the attachment between a well-meaning, loving mother and her child is not a connection made just by an umbilical cord. It is one that is formed with tender heart strings. This loving bond is forged through many years of dedication, and can cause a great deal of pain when the mother must let go of her son.

Ideally, when a son says "I do" at his wedding, the mother realizes her job is done. However, in the case of some people, the emotional, maternal ties are not so easily nor painlessly cut. This unfinished business can greatly complicate the mother-in-law/daughter-in-law dance. When the line that links the mother and her son fails to be disconnected, inevitably it becomes tangled in the feet of the dancers. Eventually someone gets stepped on or falls. How can you assist your in-law in this process of letting go or latching on?

If you're a mother-in-law...

In what area of your son and his wife's family relationship do you need to back off? List three things you can do to stay within the healthy boundaries of your relationship with your son and his family.

1.

2.

3.

Are there areas where you have never really cut the umbilical cord? If so, list them in your heart and pray now for the strength to sever the ties that shouldn't bind.

If you're a daughter-in-law...

What can you do to show your support for your mother-in-law? Keep in mind that someday you may be the hurting mother who needs to let go of a son. James 2:13 reminds us, "For judgment will be merciless to one who has shown no mercy; mercy triumphs over judgment."

What three things can you do to show your mother-in-law your love and appreciation to her as your husband's mother?

1.

2.

3.

3
Dancing Without Stepping on Toes

It's impossible to get through this life without experiencing the sting of offense. Eventually, and usually unintentionally, we will offend or be offended. The end results are feelings of hurt and anger. So the question we must face is, How will we choose to deal with these offenses when they occur?

Many of the wounds that *afflict* our hearts, as well as the ones we inadvertently *inflict* on others are a direct result of the barbs of unkind, untrue, and unnecessary words. Consequently, all of us need to be about the task of controlling our tongues. That most fleshly and sharp member of our bodies can do incredible damage. In fact, Proverbs 18:19 NLT reminds us that "it's harder to make amends with an offended friend than to capture a fortified city. Arguments separate friends like a gate locked with iron bars."

James 1:19 offers one of the keys to keeping the gate open: "Everyone must be quick to hear, slow to speak and slow to anger; for the anger of man does not achieve the righteousness of God."

Quick to hear

Slow to speak

Slow to anger

Is there an apology due your mother-in-law? Is there an apology due your daughter-in-law? Perhaps many of the wounds that the women in this chapter shared that caused years of hurt and hard feelings could have been dissipated with a simple apology.

When we choose to humble ourselves, we are not diminished in the eyes of others. Rather, humility provokes respect and, at times, makes it easier for others to yield to the work of God in their own lives. Perhaps you fear that an offered apology may be rejected. That is not your responsibility. If someone refuses to graciously accept a heartfelt appeal for forgiveness, then the burden shifts onto that person. To offer an apology should not be based on whether or not it will be received.

Isaiah 66:1-2 says:

> Thus says the LORD, "Heaven is My throne and the earth is My footstool. Where then is a house you could build for Me? And where is a place that I may rest? For My hand made all these things, thus all these things came into being," declare the LORD. "But to this one I will look, to him who is humble and contrite of spirit, and who trembles at My word."

Pay special attention to the one whom God takes notice:

1. humble
2. contrite (crushed, broken, moldable) of spirit
3. who trembles at His word

The antidote for hurt is humility. Are there some things you can do that would help heal the hurts between you and your in-law? Then, for the sake of gaining the joy of unity, go do them.

4
The Dance Floor Is Too Crowded

On the sitcom television show *Everyone Loves Raymond*, the conflicts between the mother-in-law, Marie, and daughter-in-law, Deborah, are made even more intense because they live across the street from one another. Without any prior notice, not even a polite knock on the door, they enter one another's homes unannounced and uninvited. This "close" arrangement may provide comical material for entertaining television viewing, but to anyone who has had to deal with a similar situation in real life, the reality of such broken-down boundaries is anything but a laughing matter.

Proverbs 25:17 tells us, "Let your foot *rarely* be in your neighbor's house, or he will become weary of you and hate you" (emphasis added). Could there possibly be any question as to what kind of parameters we should establish when it comes to respecting our in-laws' privacy? If a neighbor gets tired of too much visiting, just imagine how quickly family can become a nuisance. After reading the suggestions that were given by some of the women who have lived through this not-so-funny situation, are there some practical steps you can take in establishing boundaries for both you and your in-laws?

Using as your guide Proverbs 24:3, which follows, list some things you can do that will help you love and not hate your neighbor, who also happens to be your in-law.

By *wisdom* a house is built
And by *understanding* it is established
And by *knowledge* the rooms are filled
With all precious and pleasant riches
(emphasis added).

Keep in mind this truth I once heard:

We serve a God who is more than able to
change our misery into a ministry.
He is able to transform our every
test into a testimony.
And He is the Master of taking our helpless mess
and turning it into a message of hope.

Don't let the difficulty of a "too close for comfort" situation with your in-laws rob you of your joy and sense of humor. Set up the boundaries of love and live by them, even if the other one keeps stepping over the line.

5
Waltzing to Rap Music

It seems that every time I turn on the television I am met with another "Reality" show. I realize that this type of programming is really not that new. In fact, the very first one that I can remember was produced back in the 60s with the very popular "Smile! You're on Candid Camera." However, these modern-day shows have taken on a different, even disturbing twist.

One of the most popular programs now, and I have to admit that I've viewed it from time to time, is the show "Extreme Makeover." On this particular show they select individuals who are not happy with their outward appearance. For some they want to fix what is a considered a culturally unacceptable problem. Perhaps it's a big nose, small chin, or protruding ears that stands between them and complete and utter happiness. While for others it is the ravages of disease that they seek to remedy. One very grateful woman had her breast reconstructed after having lost it to cancer. But most often it is the scars of time, more commonly known as wrinkles, that people want eradicated. What I find most upsetting is that most of the people having the nips, tucks, and lifts are younger than me. It sends me running to the bathroom mirror to see if I should be the next contestant.

Among the many noticeable differences between our generation and that of our parents, one is certainly the growing willingness of the younger generation to undergo the risk and pain of cosmetic surgery. Of course, for decades women (and sometimes men) have "gone under the knife" to correct flaws and try to recapture the fountain of youth, but never in the numbers and never to the degree of invasive procedures that they do now.

Mothers-in-law and daughters-in-law who find themselves looking at life through different viewfinders as a result of coming from different generations need to beware of the lines that may scar their lives. It is not the creases that appear on our faces that tend to distort and make ugly our relationships, but the more important wrinkles in the lines of communication and the willingness to give a "lift" to those with whom we may not see eye to eye.

As women who care about rediscovering and reestablishing the lines of communication between the generations, take some time to think about some constructive ways you can bridge that gap. Then list three of those things you can do that will help make a positive connection with your in-law.

1.

2.

3.

6
Square Dancing on a Round Floor

Families are like snowflakes—unique. Even those who seem similar and compatible to one another, once you get to know them, will reveal themselves to be distinct from other families. Being different is not a bad thing at all. However, it can be rather challenging to the one who is expected to adapt herself to and become an intricate part of a family that is not only unfamiliar, but also does things and thinks in a different way.

Differences in individuals as well as family units are like the spices we use to flavor foods we enjoy. The addition of herbs and seasonings creates a unique blend that enhances what would otherwise be a bland mix. Think of chili for instance. This dish is made up of beans, ground meat, and tomatoes. There's nothing extraordinary about that combination until you add the zing of chili powder. As everyone knows, though, spicy food is a tasty treat, but it has its hazards. It may produce discomforting indigestion or raging heartburn.

The same can be true when families are blended by marriage. The mixture of "spicy" personalities might upset the tummy. But there's good news. There are antacids that can quiet the social rumble. They are *appreciation, acceptance,* and *affection.*

Appreciation

Drawing from the information and ideas in chapter 6, list three things you can do right away to show your appreciation for your in-law. Include an intended date to have accomplished these deeds of kindness. Be sure to follow through!

1. _____ date:_____

2. _____ date:_____

3. _____ date:_____

Acceptance

Spiritual and personal maturity demands that we understand and accept the distinct roles the mother of the son and the wife of the son occupy. Both the mother-in-law and daughter-in-law are expected and required to regard with honor their unique places in the family.

As a mother-in-law, list three things you can do that will honor your son's wife and show her you accept her God-given place in the family.

1.

2.

3.

As a daughter-in-law, list three things you can do that will honor your husband's mother and show her that you accept her place in the family.

1.

2.

3.

Affection

The end result of showing appreciation and acceptance is to experience more of a sense of affection between in-laws.

Since love is an action verb and is defined in 1 Corinthians 13 as being patient and kind, list three things that you can do that will demonstrate a more patient attitude.

1.

2.

3.

List three acts of kindness can you do that will show your love for your in-law.

1.

2.

3.

The end result of showing appreciation and acceptance is experiencing more of a sense of affection between in-laws.

7
When You Hear a Different Beat

A sincere love for Christ, without a doubt, is the most important bond that cements a family together. In Colossians 1:17, we read that in Christ all things hold together. On that list of "all things" are, of course, families. Even as our common bond in Christ can be the "divine glue" that bonds us together, not sharing that same love leaves us vulnerable to the stress fractures of life.

Mothers-in-law and daughters-in-law can refortify their love cords by sharing a desire to know and love God. In chapter 7 we looked at what Jesus did for us for the purpose of embracing the joy of knowing Him. To highlight what great love He has for us, consider this story from history.

> During Oliver Cromwell's reign as lord protector of England a young soldier was sentenced to die. The girl to whom he was engaged pleaded with Cromwell to spare the life of her beloved, but to no avail. The young man was to be executed when the curfew bell sounded, but when the sexton repeatedly pulled the rope the bell made no sound. The girl had climbed into the belfry and wrapped herself around the clapper so that it could not strike the bell. Her body

was smashed and battered, but she did not let go until the clapper stopped swinging. She managed to climb down, bruised and bleeding, to meet those awaiting the execution. When she explained what she had done, Cromwell commuted the sentence. A poet beautifully recorded the story as follows:

> At his feet she told her story,
> showed her hands all bruised and torn
> And her sweet young face still haggard
> with the anguish it had worn
> Touched his heart with sudden pity
> lit his eyes with misty light
> "Go, your lover lives," said Cromwell
> "Curfew will not ring tonight."[1]

The beating this future daughter-in-law took to save the life of her beloved is merely a faint picture of what Christ has done for us. Although we were guilty and deserving of death, Christ wrapped Himself around us and took our beating. Isaiah foretold the painful sacrifice Jesus would make on our behalf: "He was wounded for our transgressions, he was bruised for our iniquities: the chastisement of our peace was upon him; and with his stripes we are healed" (Isaiah 53:5 KJV). And the apostle Paul confirms that the sacrifice was made: "God demonstrates His own love toward us, in that while we were yet sinners, Christ died for us" (Romans 5:8).

When we fully understand what Christ has done for us, we can't help but love Him and want to serve Him. The love that Christ has shown us is the bridge that spans the spiritual gap between in-laws. As long as Christ is the center of our attention, then all insignificant disagreements (and anything other than who and what Christ is and did are, indeed, insignificant) can be overcome.

What do you need to do now that you more fully understand who Christ is and what He has done for you? If the Spirit of God is speaking to your heart, then stop now and pray. Perhaps this simple prayer will assist you.

> Dear loving, heavenly Father,
> I acknowledge that I have sinned.
> I've tried to live my life independently of You.
> My ignorance and pride have kept me from reaching out to You.
> I believe in my heart that Jesus has taken my beating
> and has paid the price for my sin through
> His death on the cross.
> I believe that death was not strong enough to hold Him down,
> and, on the third day, He got up out of the grave.
> I ask You, Lord Jesus, to come into my life and
> take over the controls.
> I surrender everything to You.
> Please forgive me and lead me in how to live.
> In Jesus' name. Amen.

If you prayed this prayer and you accept Christ as your Savior, I urge you to go now and share your decision with someone who shares your faith in the Lord. Perhaps that person is the in-law who may have been the one who has encouraged you to do so. The healing this can bring about could very well transform your relationship.

8
Boxers Dance, Too

Perhaps one reason God compared His people to sheep (see Psalm 23; Isaiah 53:6) is because they have a tendency to be very baaad! Okay, seriously now, there's a challenging but doable solution to the conflicts that arise between in-laws. There would be no need for the three keys I shared to overcoming strife, if we would live according to Philippians 2. In this ancient passage, Paul writes, "Make my joy complete by being of the same mind, maintaining the same love, united in spirit, intent on one purpose" (verse 2). What a wonderful goal for your current relationship! But as noble as this goal may be, how does a mother-in-law or daughter-in-law get to the place of such harmonious unity when each of them has to contend with her basic sinful nature to be willful and stubborn? Once again, Paul has the answer to this hard question.

If verse two of Philippians 2 gives us the desired destination for our relationship, then the following verses offer the road map to that blessed place:

> Do nothing from selfishness or empty conceit,
> but with humility of mind regard one another
> as more important than yourselves; do not
> merely look out for your own personal inter-
> ests, but also for the interests of others. Have
> this attitude in yourselves which was also in

Christ Jesus....[who took] the form of a bond-
servant" (verses 3-5,7).

Living according to these principles will help us avoid the
unpleasantness of conflict. However, what practical things can
you do if the other party refuses to live according to God's
Word? As you answer this question, keep the "three keeps" in
mind: *Keep* your distance, *keep* your tongue, *keep* on smiling.

Now, list at least two additional things you can do to help
minimize the conflicts between you and your in-law.

1.

2.

Since you cannot change the other person, take some
moments to write down some ways you can change yourself
that could help lessen the stress of your situation. Then, write
down some of the things you plan to change.

_____

_____

_____

_____

_____

_____

_____

_____

_____

_____

9
Trading Partners

When the religious leaders asked Jesus to give His interpretation on the subject of divorce, they were trying to catch Him contradicting the Law of Moses. However, instead of agreeing or disagreeing with their perceived ideas, He began by reminding them of the original purpose of marriage. He answered the Pharisees' inquiry by stating that divorce was not even supposed to be an option. He stated, "Because of your hardness of heart [Moses] wrote you this commandment. But from the beginning of creation, God made them male and female. For this reason a man shall leave his father and mother, and the two shall become one flesh; so they are no longer two, but one flesh. What therefore God has joined together, let no man separate" (Mark 10:5-9).

Divorce is a remedy to a problem that is not supposed to exist. As Christians, the last thing in God's plan for us is to have hard, stony hearts toward those we have committed to love and live with until our deaths. However, the sad fact remains that many dedicated Christians are left to make sense of the senselessness of divorce because the ones who promised to love and cherish them changed their minds. How do we make sense out of something that is not supposed to be? Not only can you not find logic in the illogical or order in the disorder of divorce, but any solution that may be suggested will, at best, be inadequate. Still, I offer the following encouragements.

If you are faced with the painful sting of divorce as a mother-in-law or as a daughter-in-law, then I pray that God will guide you to the quiet peace that comes from a heart that is willing to…

- ⊙ guard against assigning blame.

- ⊙ guard against accusing words.

- ⊙ guard against acting unkindly.

If, however, you have dropped your guard in these areas, today is the day of healing. May I urge you to begin by asking yourself these questions.

- ⊙ Do you owe your in-law an apology?

- ⊙ Have you assigned blame to your in-law without knowing all the facts?

- ⊙ Have you thrown the barbs of accusing words into the heart of your in-law?

- ⊙ Have you done things out of hurt and disappointment that were unkind and undeserving?

If the answer to any of these questions is yes, the following prayer will be appropriate.

Dear God,
You know the hurt and the harm that has been done to all of us,
through this tragedy of divorce.
With full regret, I fear that I have contributed to the
destruction of others by letting my guard down.
I have become part of the problem, instead of the solution.
Please forgive the additional damage
that I have done to those I am to love.

I now ask You to forgive me my sins, even as I forgive those
who have hurt me. Father, please show
me how to seek forgiveness from those I have hurt.

You are the God of second chances.
You are full of mercy and truth.
In You and You alone is peace and healing.
In Jesus' name. Amen.

Notes

Chapter 2: Who Is Supposed to Lead?

1. Steve Chapman, 2003. Used by permission.

2. Steve Chapman, *The Arrow and the Bow*, Dawn Treader Music/SESAC, 1983. Used by permission.

3. Steve Chapman, *Dance with the One*. Used by permission.

Chapter 7: When You Hear a Different Beat

1. "Sermons We See" has been attributed to various authors, including Edgar Guest.

2. Louis Barbieri, *Moody Gospel: Mark Commentary* (Chicago: Moody, 1995), p. 124.

Chapter 8: Boxers Dance, Too

1. *To His Mother*, author unknown.

STUDY GUIDE
Chapter 7: When You Hear a Different Beat

1. John MacArthur, *The MacArthur New Testament Commentary of 1 Corinthians* (Chicago: Moody, 1984), p. 353.

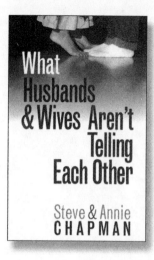

WHAT HUSBANDS AND WIVES
AREN'T TELLING EACH OTHER
Steve and Annie Chapman

What is the greatest challenge of your marriage? What is your greatest concern regarding financial health? What do you and your spouse do for fun? Exploring these and other questions, Steve and Annie Chapman draw on their 28 years of married life, God's Word, and a survey of almost 500 couples to explore foundational conversations that highlight the truths upon which successful marriages are built. As you examine real-life situations, you'll discover the keys to making marriage more satisfying:

* finding spiritual wholeness

* creating a partnership in love, cooperation, and mutual submission

* realizing the importance of flexibility

* recapturing the laughter lost in daily living

* developing a mature love that will last a lifetime

As you explore vital topics seldom discussed, your marriage will become deeper and more fulfilling.

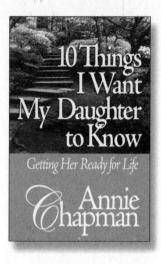

10 THINGS I WANT MY DAUGHTER
TO KNOW
Annie Chapman

What a blessing God has given you...a beautiful daughter! As you gaze into her future, what values and life skills would you like her to have? What activities can you do together to help her become a woman of God? Drawing on her experiences, the wisdom of God's Word, and insights from other mothers, Annie Chapman highlights 10 essential truths and how to share them with your daughter. You'll also discover guidance for developing faith, discernment, trust, and integrity from the lives of women in the Bible. Speaking from her heart, Annie candidly reveals the ups and downs of motherhood to help you navigate the sometimes tricky yet always fulfilling role of "Mom."

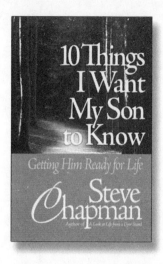

10 THINGS I WANT MY SON
TO KNOW
Steve Chapman

Fatherhood. What an amazing gift from God! Being a dad requires love, humor, wisdom...and nerves of steel. And that's only the beginning. Turning to the only "manual" that comes with children, Steve Chapman shares his top-10 principles drawn from the Bible's wisdom and practical experience that helped him raise a son dedicated to the Lord. Whether you're just starting out on the "papa" road or have traveled part of the distance, you'll appreciate the practical information, hands-on suggestions, and often humorous examples Steve shares to help you raise a son who will be a man of God and a man of honor.